Hamilton Ontario Book 3 in Colour Photos, Saving Our History One Photo at a Time

Photography
by Barbara Raué
2014

Series Name:
Cruising Ontario

Book 89: Hamilton Book 3

Cover photo: 105 East Avenue South

Series Name: Cruising Ontario
Saving Our History One Photo at a Time
in colour photos

Other Books by Barbara Raue

Coins of Gold

Arrows, Indians and Love

The Life and Times of Barbara
Volume 1: Inventions That Have Enhanced My Life
Volume 2: Entertainment That I Have Enjoyed
Volume 3: East Coast Trips
Volume 4: Olympics Have Always Intrigued Me
Volume 5: Wonders of the World
Volume 6: Caribbean Cruises We Have Enjoyed
Volume 7: Animals
Volume 8: Storms and Other Major Disasters in My Lifetime
Volume 9: Wars, Terrorist Attacks and Major Disasters

The Cromwell Family Book

Laura Secord Discovered

Visit Barbara's website to view all of her books
http://barbararaue.ca

In 1784, thousands of United Empire Loyalists settled in Upper Canada (what is now southern Ontario). Iroquois loyal to Britain arrived from the United States and were settled on reserves. Between 1788 and 1793, the townships at the Head-of-the-Lake were surveyed and named.

John Ryckman, born in Barton township (where present day downtown Hamilton is), described the area in 1803 as he remembered it: "The city in 1803 was all forest. The shores of the bay were difficult to reach or see because they were hidden by a thick, almost impenetrable mass of trees and undergrowth... Bears ate pigs, so settlers warred on bears. Wolves gobbled sheep and geese, so they hunted and trapped wolves. They also held organized raids on rattlesnakes on the mountainside. There was plenty of game. Many a time have I seen a deer jump the fence into my back yard, and there were millions of pigeons which we clubbed as they flew low."

Hamilton, the centre of a densely populated and industrialized region, is located in Southern Ontario on the western part of Lake Ontario. Hamilton Harbour marks the northern limit of the city, and the Niagara Escarpment runs through the middle of the city bisecting the city into "upper" and "lower" parts. There are over one hundred waterfalls and cascades within the city, most of which are on or near the Bruce Trail as it winds through the Niagara Escarpment.

Two steel manufacturing companies, Stelco and Dofasco, were formed in 1910 and 1912, and Procter & Gamble opened a manufacturing plant in 1914. The Pigott Building was the city's first high-rise building constructed in 1929. McMaster University moved from Toronto to Hamilton, an airport was built in 1940, a Studebaker assembly line started in 1948, the Burlington Bay Skyway Bridge was built in 1958, and the first Tim Horton's store opened in 1964.

Table of Contents

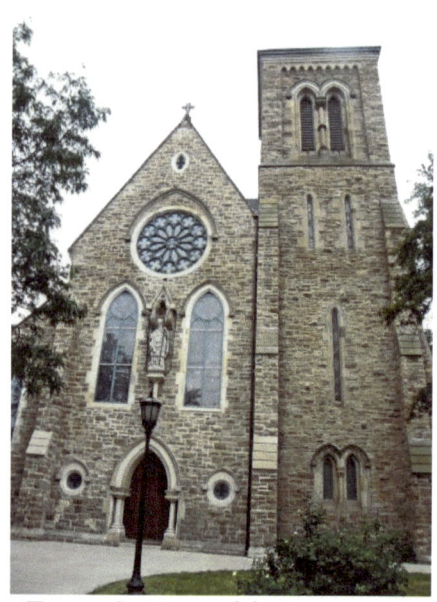

440 King Street East - St. Patrick's Roman Catholic Church - Gothic Revival architecture built 1875

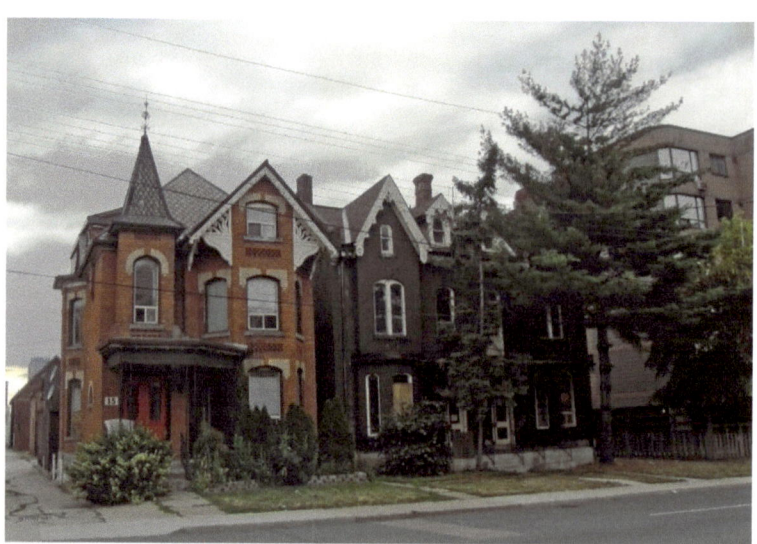

15 Victoria Avenue North – Gothic Revival, fretwork, verge board trim

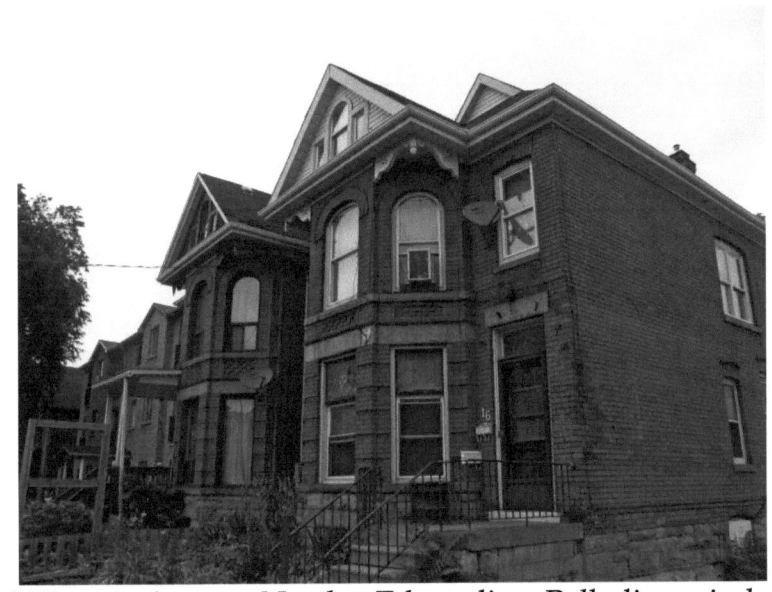

16 Victoria Avenue North – Edwardian, Palladian window

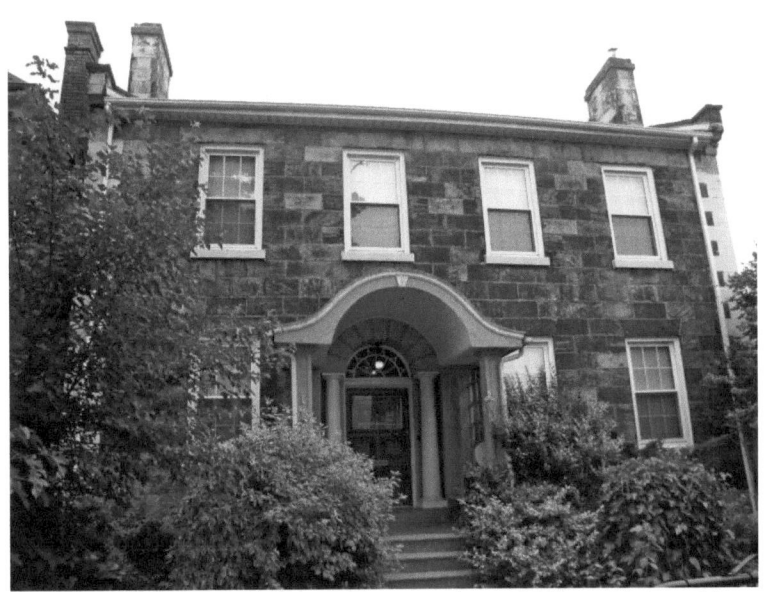

158 Mary Street (corner of Cannon) - William Pring House
Built 1851

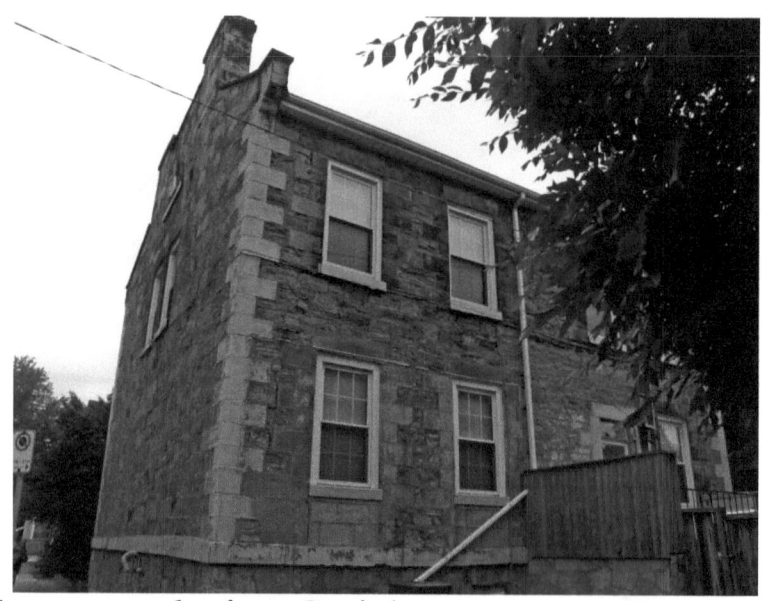

A rare example of pre-Confederation stone architecture in Hamilton; corner quoins

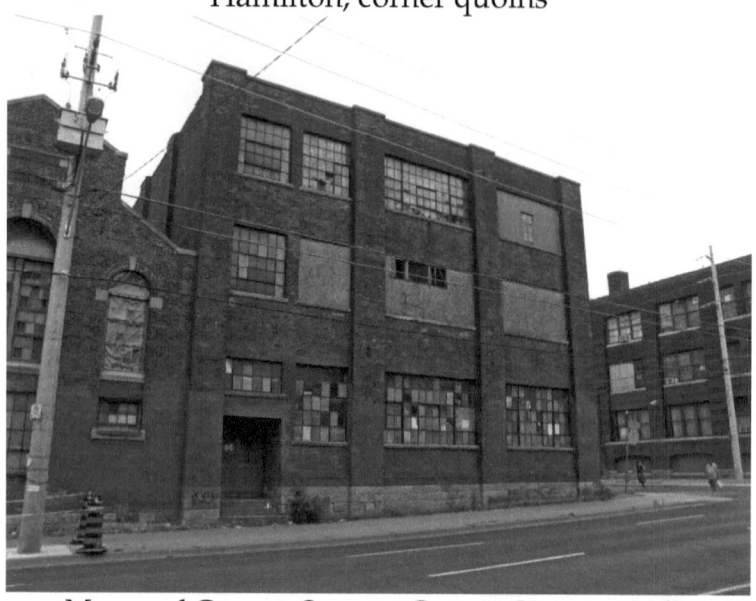

Mary and Cannon Streets - Cannon Knitting Mills
Built between 1854 and 1950
Cannon Knitting made hosiery, school curtains, bedding for hotels
and milled cotton into big bolts of fabric.

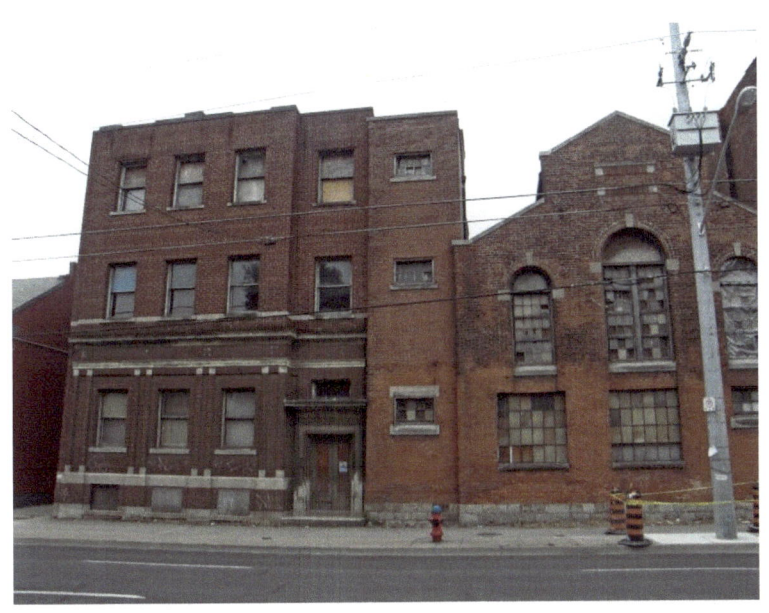

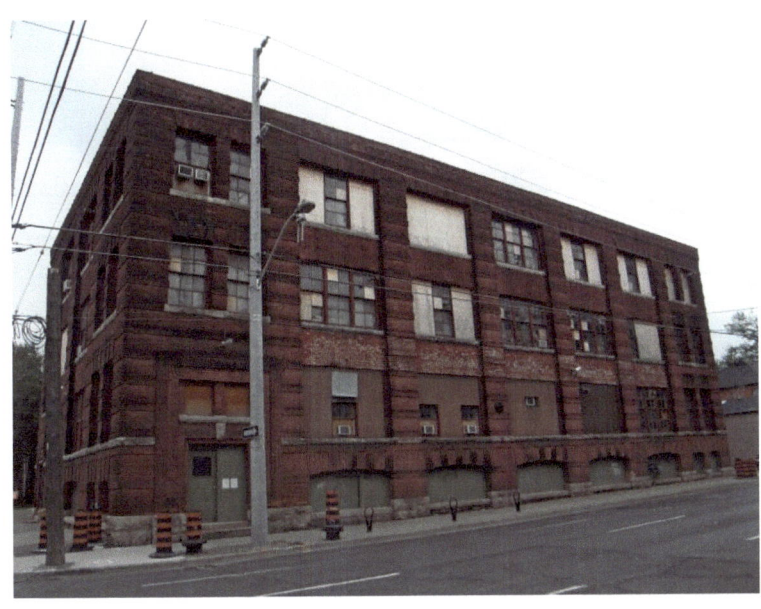

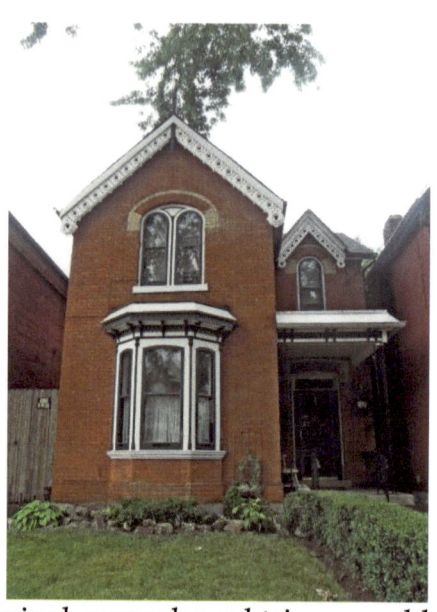

#17 – Gothic Revival, verge board trim on gables, bay window

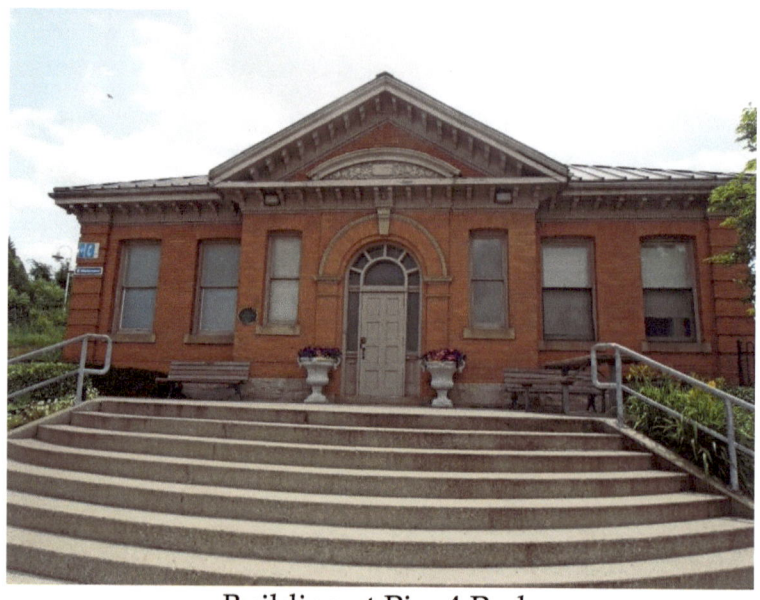

Building at Pier 4 Park

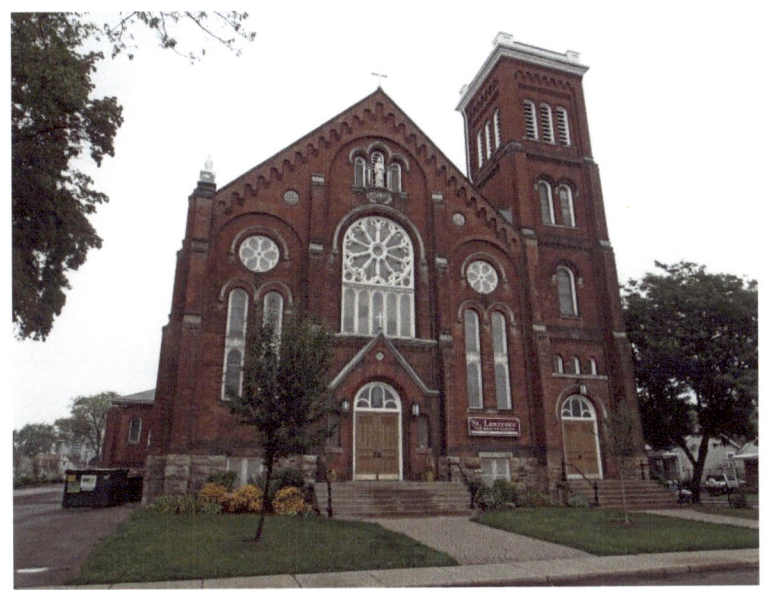

475 Mary Street (corner of Picton Street)
St. Lawrence the Martyr Church A.D. 1890
Rose window, buttresses, bell tower

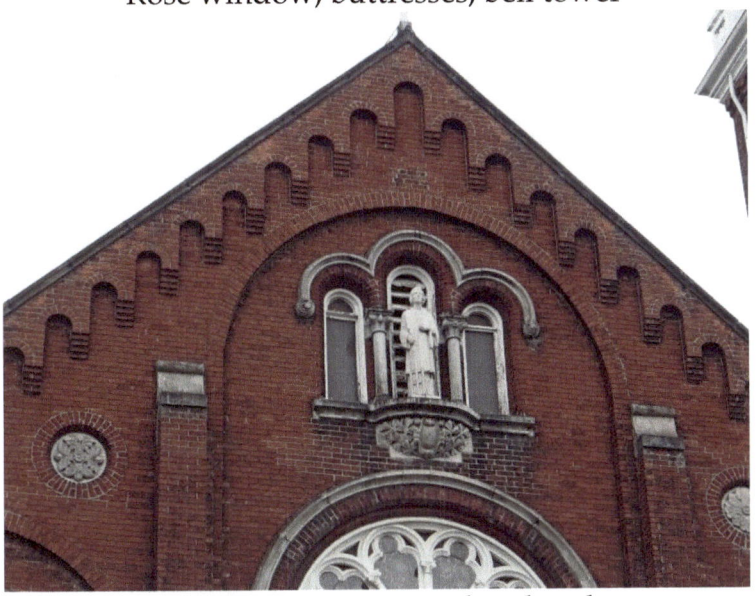

Corbelled dentils, window hoods

Land's Inlet

Land's Inlet started as a stream valley but widened due to changing lake levels and erosion. When the first settlers arrived in Hamilton the inlet extended 1.7 km inland from the harbour and was probably at least 30 metres wide near this site.

Land's Inlet was named for Robert Land, a United Empire Loyalist who was one of Hamilton's first settlers. He risked his life as a dispatch bearer for the British during the American Revolution, was captured, escaped and made his way over the border into Upper Canada. After learning that his home in Pennsylvania had been burned and his wife and children were thought dead, Land worked tirelessly to survive alone in the wilderness east of Land's Inlet. Happily, Land's family had secretly fled Pennsylvania the day before their house was burned. Robert's wife Phoebe searched for him and in 1786 the family was reunited after an eight year separation.

Before the development of this part of Hamilton, Land's Inlet was a rich wildlife area with vegetation lining the banks, and it appears to have been navigable by small craft to a point near the intersection of Wilson Street and Ferguson Avenue.

In 1835, the Hamilton Agricultural Works was built on the east shore of Land's Inlet, probably using its water to produce the first Canadian-made threshing machines. The company operated for over 100 years under various names, including as the Sawyer-Massey Company Limited from 1910 until after World War II. The Sawyer-Massey building still stands on Wellington Street.

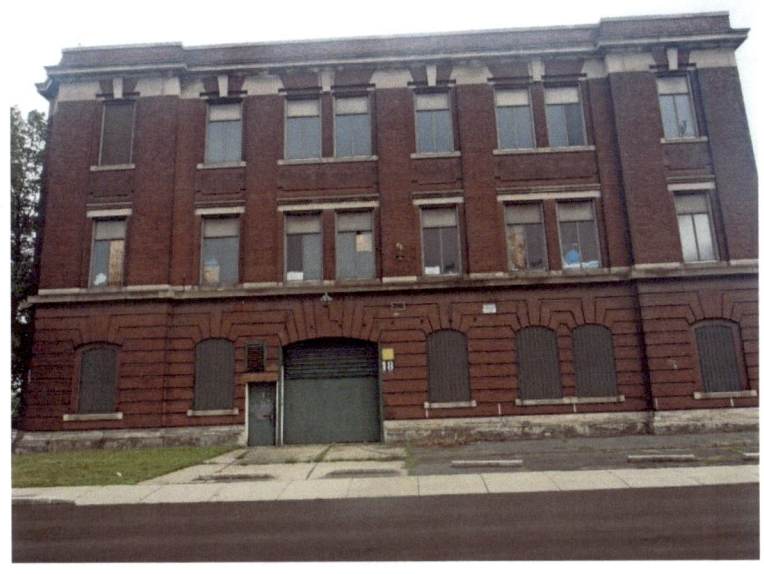

The Sawyer-Massey building

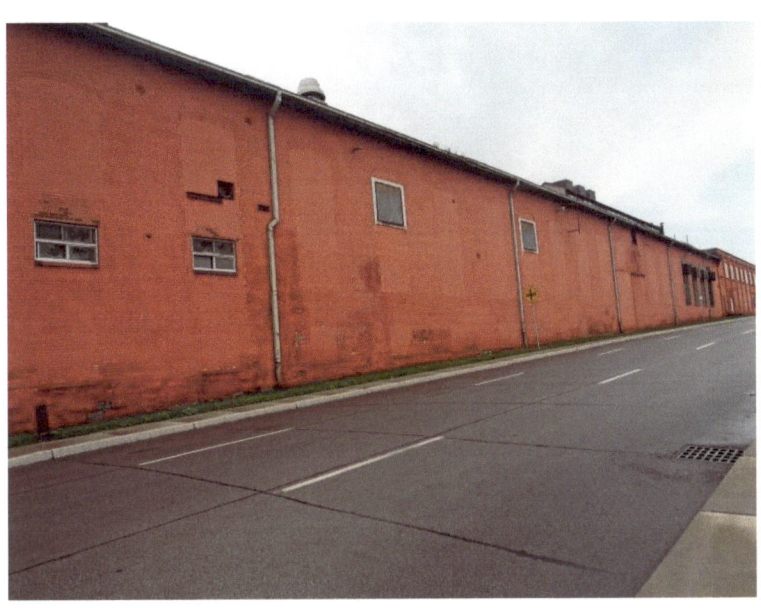

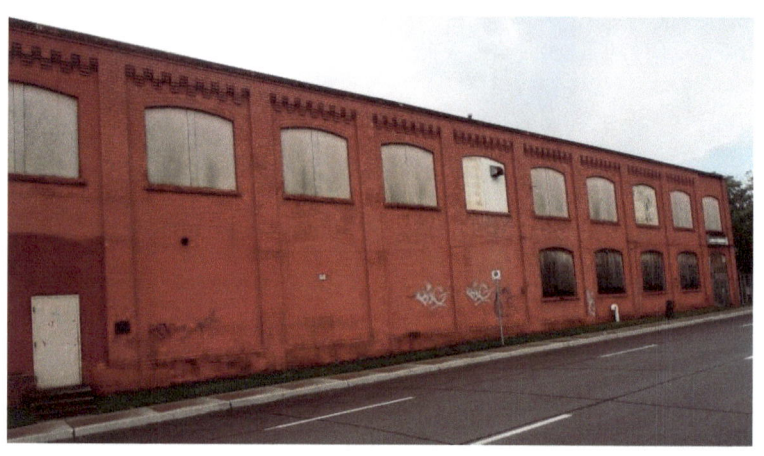

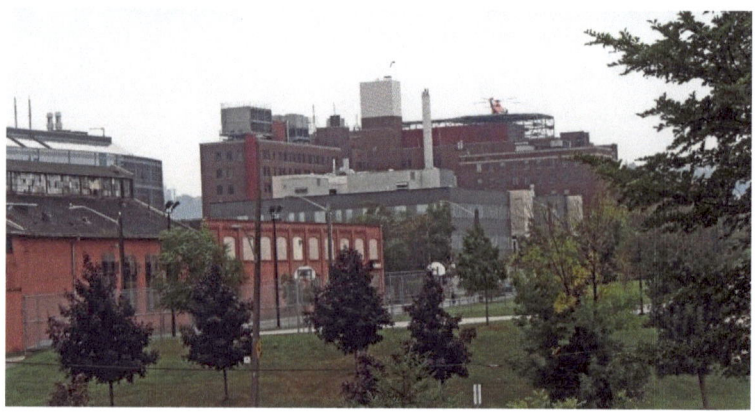

With increasing industrialization came the railway. By 1874 rail lines ran adjacent to Land's Inlet and crossed the inlet on a trestle near its mouth. The inlet was gradually filled in during the late 19th and early 20th centuries and used for industrial, transportation and residential purposes. Even though 9 metres of fill were added, the former location of the inlet can still be seen in the contours of the land.

The Plastimet Fire

Directly across the rail line is the site of Hamilton's worst ever industrial fire. From July 9th through 12th 1997, the Plastimet fire consumed a 7,400 square metre industrial building being used to store plastics. Much of this neighbourhood was evacuated and toxic fumes and fallout raised serious concerns for local residents and firefighters. The site was capped and in 2004 with support from the Rotary Club of Hamilton it was transformed into Jackie Washington Rotary Park.

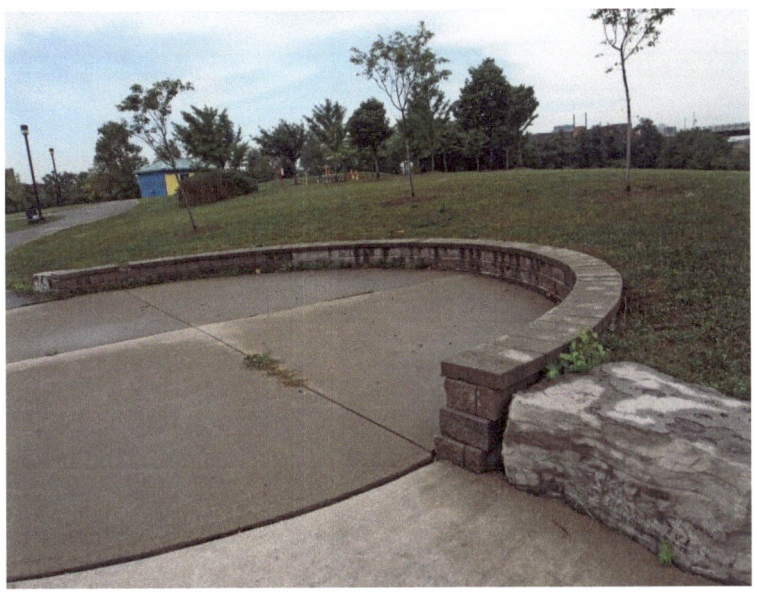

The Land's Inlet Nature Project

Neighbours came together to help turn the former industrial land into a place for nature, a place where birds and butterflies can thrive and where children can experience nature near their homes. Tons of garbage and recyclables had to be removed before planting could begin. 130 native trees and shrubs and over 1750 native flowers and prairie plants were planted. Planting a wide variety of suitable species is important to successful naturalization. Forty-one different species were planted here. This range of flowering plants means that something is always in bloom for bees, butterflies and people to enjoy.

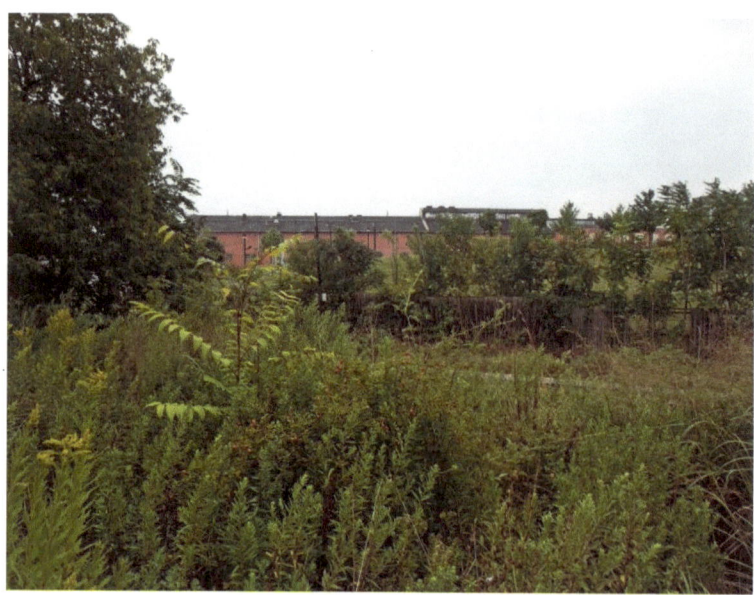

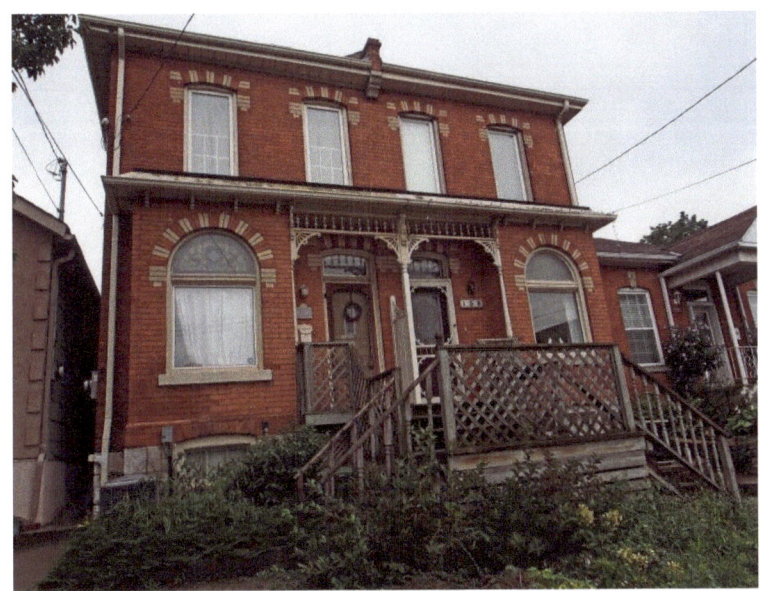

158-160 Simcoe Street East – Italianate, dichromatic brickwork

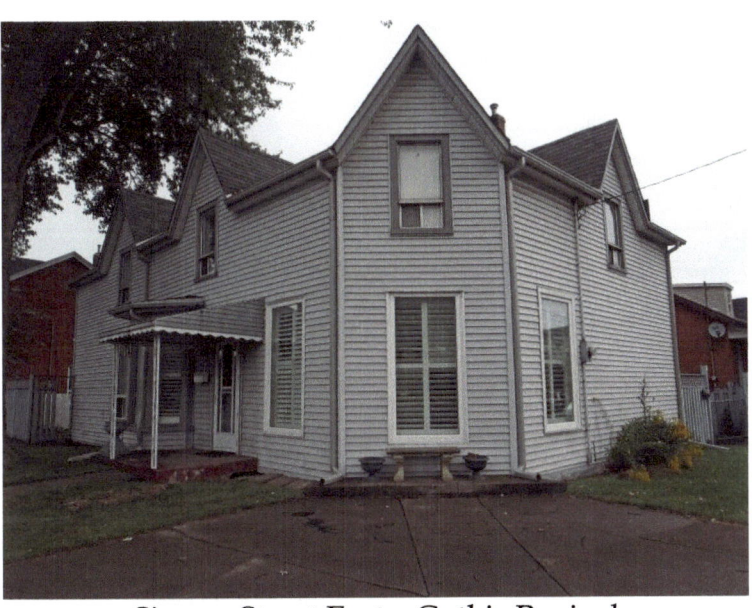

Simcoe Street East – Gothic Revival

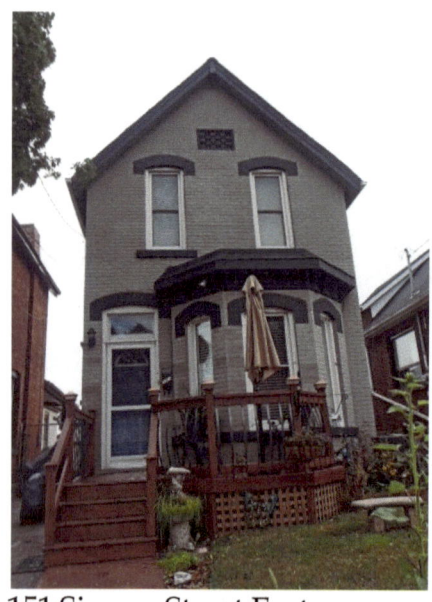

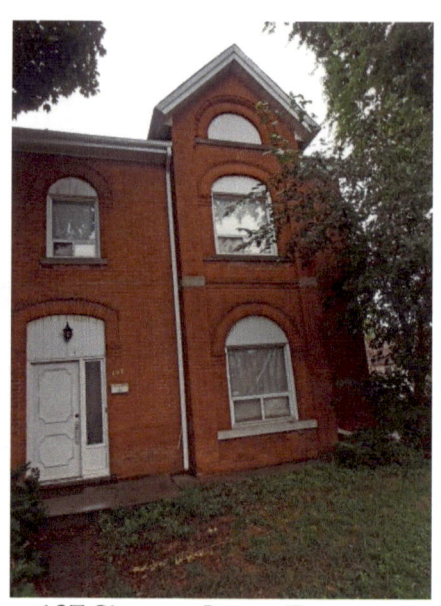

151 Simcoe Street East
Gothic Revival

107 Simcoe Street East

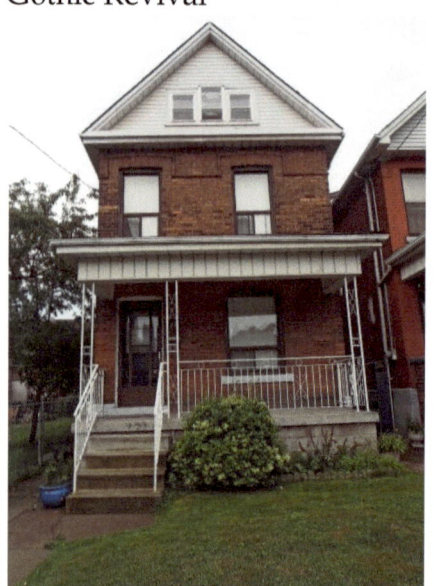

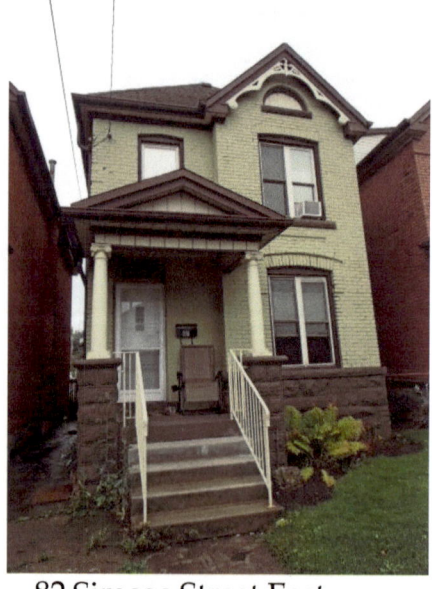

88 Simcoe Street East
Edwardian
Palladian window

82 Simcoe Street East
Gothic Revival, pediment
verge board trim on gable

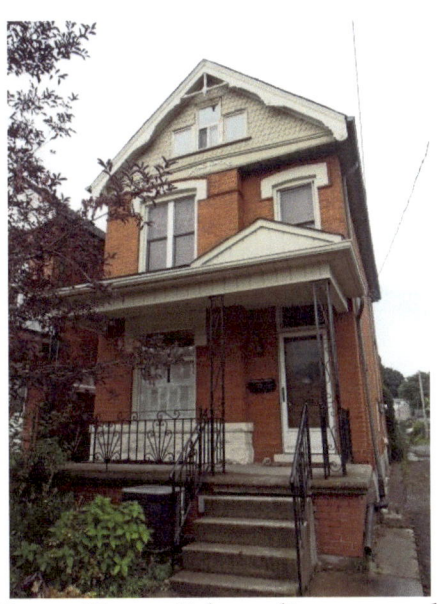

76 Simcoe Street East – Edwardian, verge board trim,
pediment above verandah, Palladian window

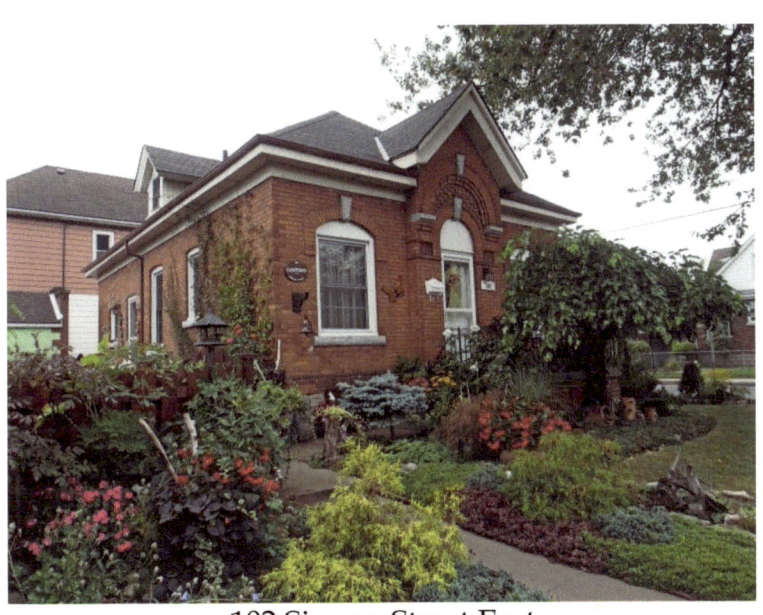

102 Simcoe Street East

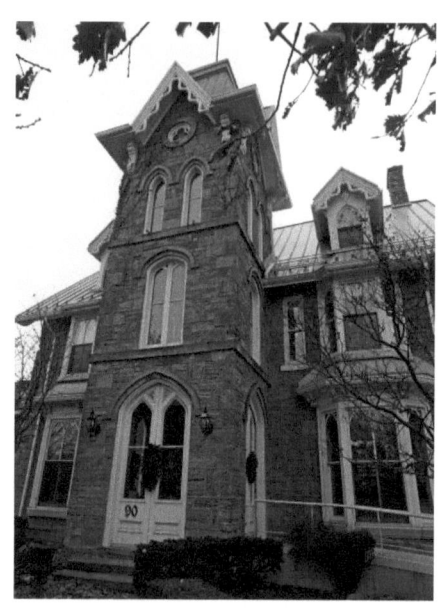

90 Stinson Street

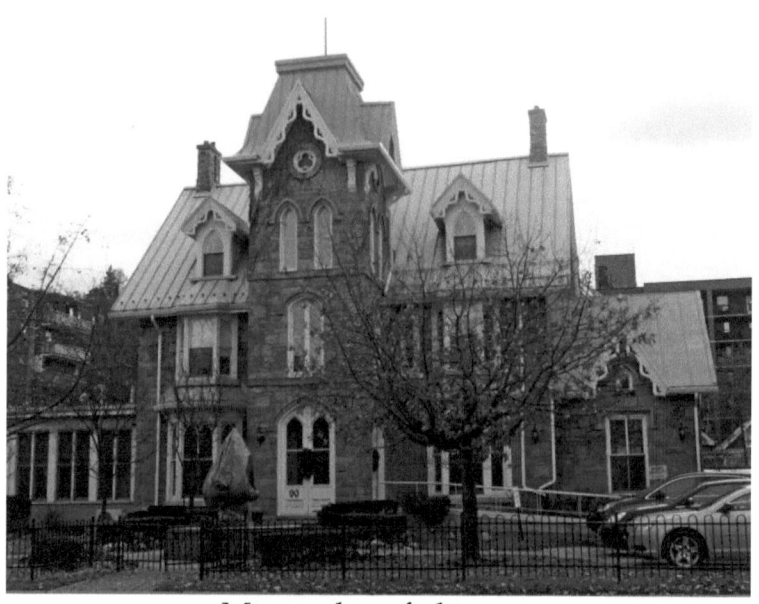

Mansard-roofed tower

Frederick William Fearman was the son of a shoemaker who emigrated from England in 1833 with his parents at the age of eight.

He started his business with a store selling smoked and salted meats on Hughson Street between King and King William, moved to a MacNab Street North location near the farmers' market, and eventually expanded to become W. Fearman Packing Company Limited, with a large factory at Rebecca Street and Ferguson Avenue on the Grand Trunk Railway line. The company slaughtered, hung, salted, smoked and canned pork, beef, veal and lamb for shipment around the world.

Fearman built his mansion, "Ivey Lodge", at 90 Stinson Street in 1863. It is three-storey, limestone block with a Mansard-roofed tower as its front entrance; it has bay and arched windows, dormers, verge board trim, and a green metal roof.

Fearman used his influence to help establish Hamilton as a major centre in Canada's early days. He was a philanthropist who fought for the city's first waterworks in 1855 and led the fight to buy Dundurn Castle and park to save it from land developers. Fearman served on the Board of Education, city council, the library board, and was a member of the Hamilton Association for the Advancement of Literature, Science and Art. Fearman died at age 81 in 1906.

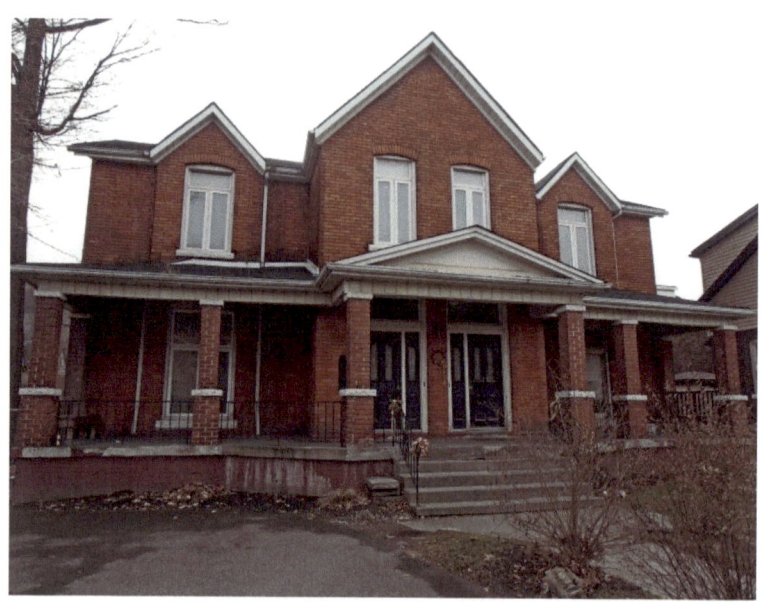

110 Stinson Street – Gothic Revival

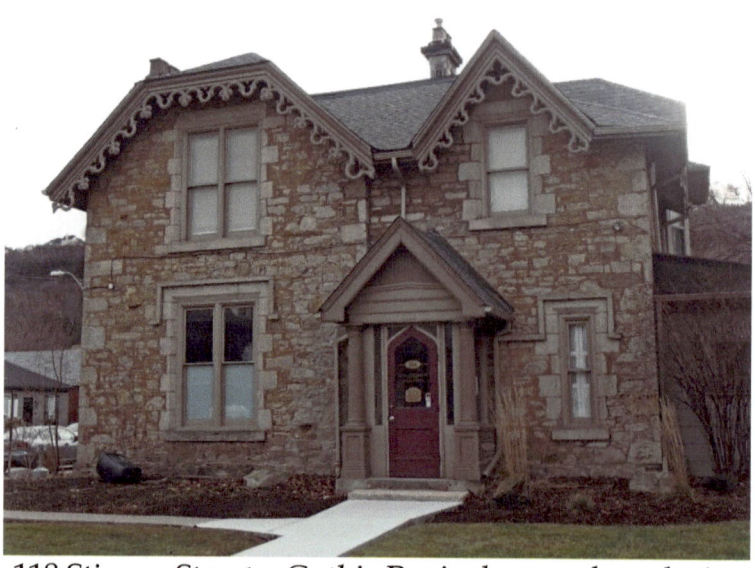

118 Stinson Street – Gothic Revival, verge board trim

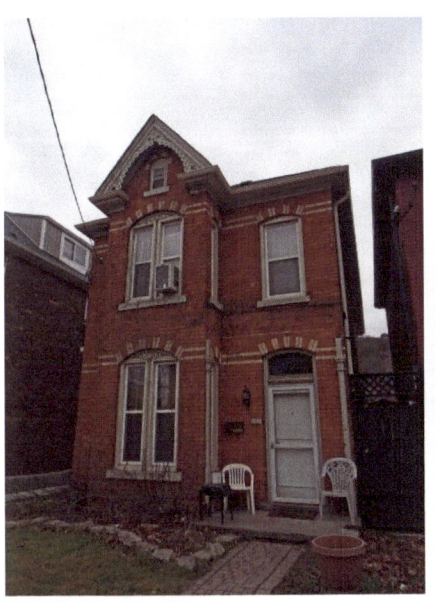

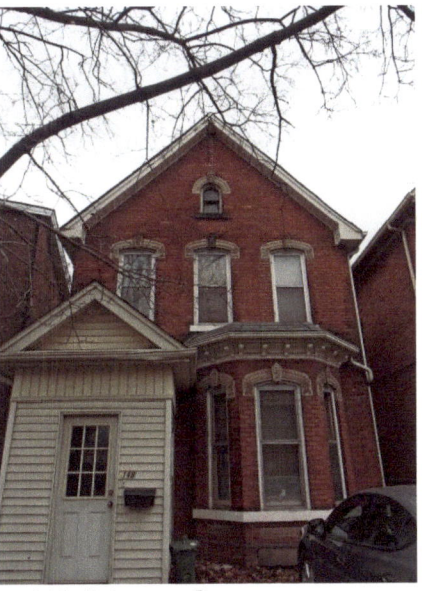

154 Stinson Street
Banding,
dichromatic brickwork

148 Stinson Street
Gothic Revival
bay window

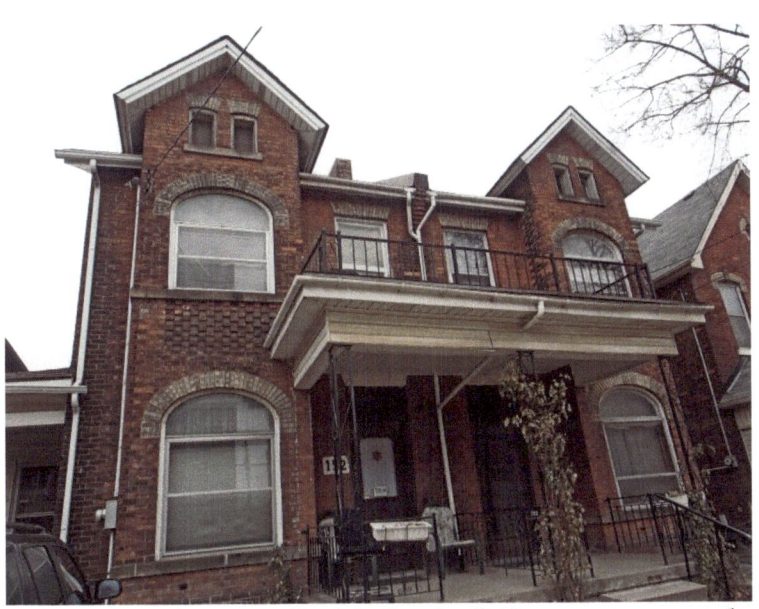

152 Stinson Street – Gothic Revival, Romanesque style
window arches, second floor balcony

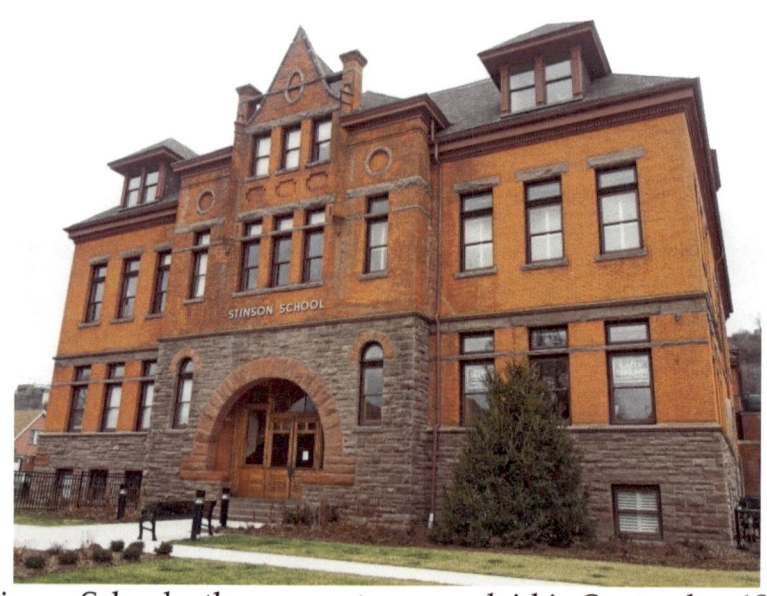

Stinson School – the cornerstone was laid in September 1894 and opened in May 1895 – built of brick and brown Credit Valley stone – beautiful arched entrance – it closed as a school in 2009 and was converted into condominium lofts

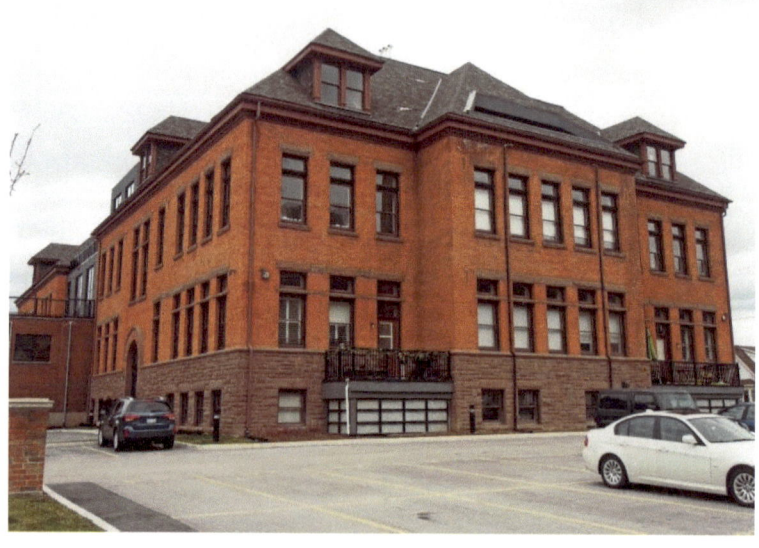

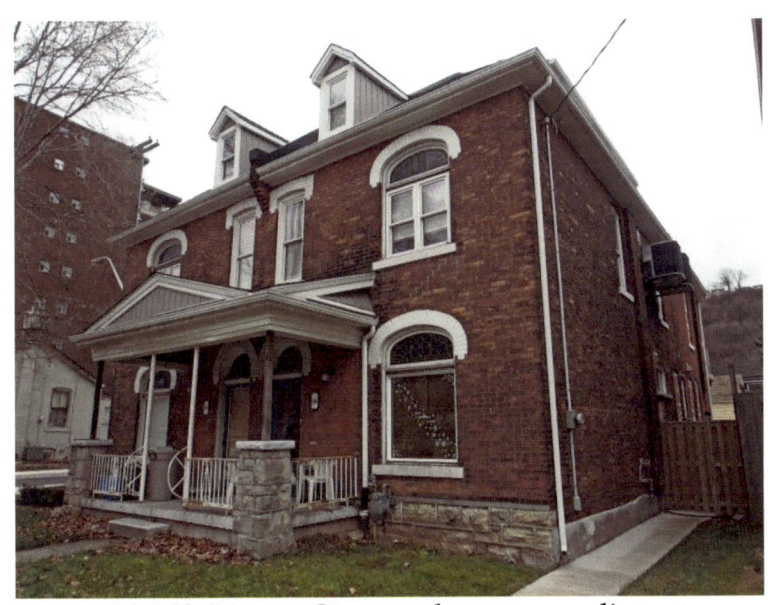

166-168 Stinson Street – dormers, pediment

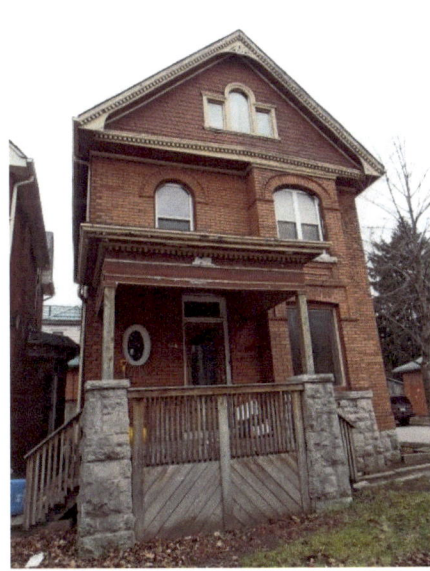

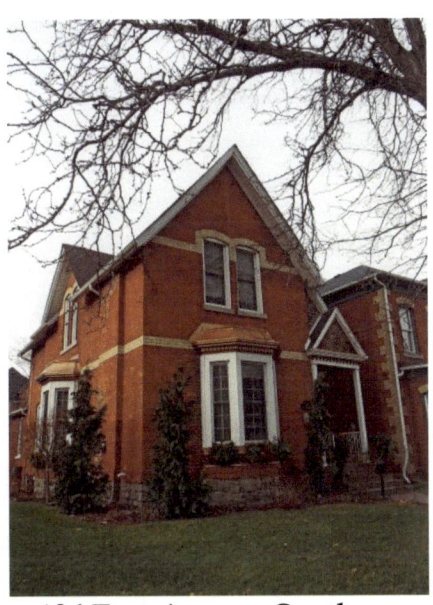

146 Stinson Street
Edwardian, Palladian window

136 East Avenue South
Gothic Revival, banding,
Bay window

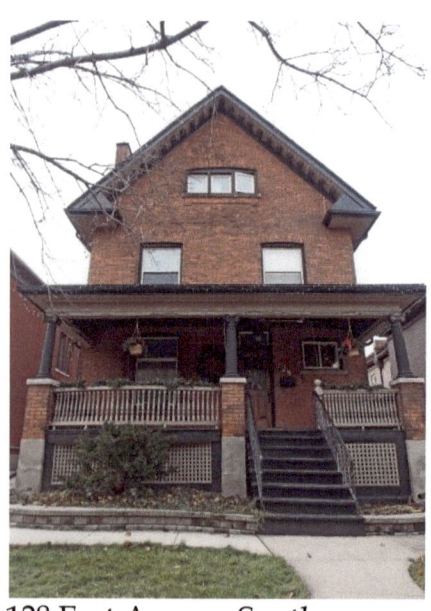

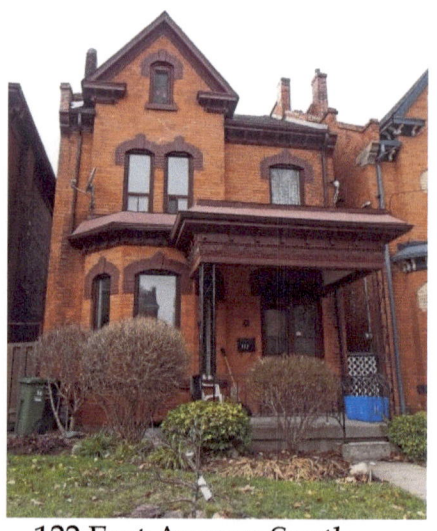

128 East Avenue South
Gothic Revival, cornice return

122 East Avenue South
cornice return on gable

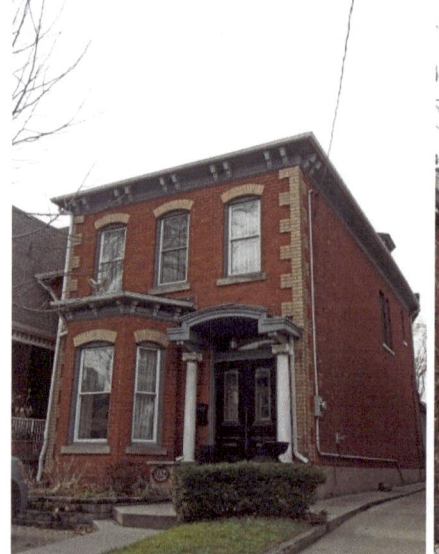

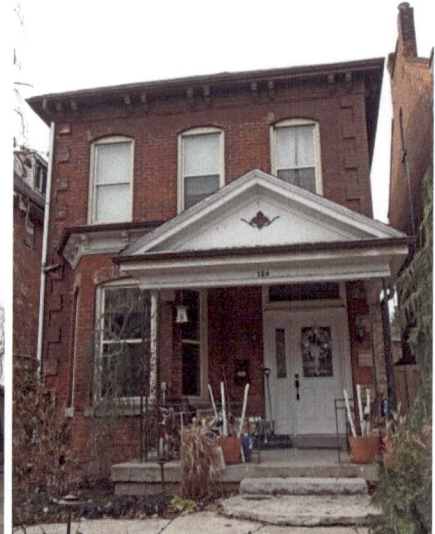

132 East Avenue South
Italianate, cornice brackets, bay windows
Corner quoins

124 East Avenue South
pediment

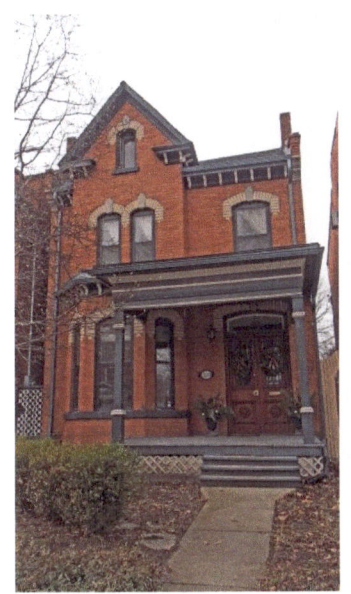

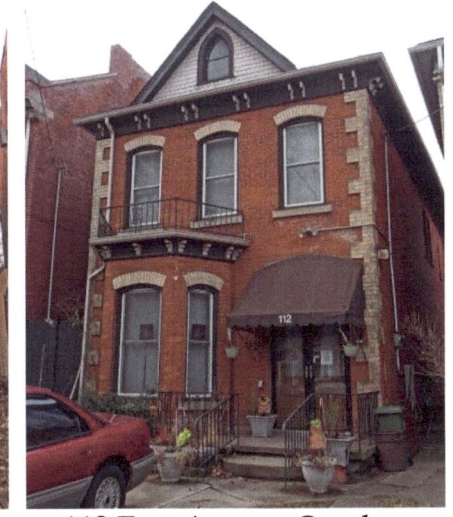

120 East Avenue South
Cornice return
Cornice brackets

112 East Avenue South
corner quoins, bay window
cornice brackets

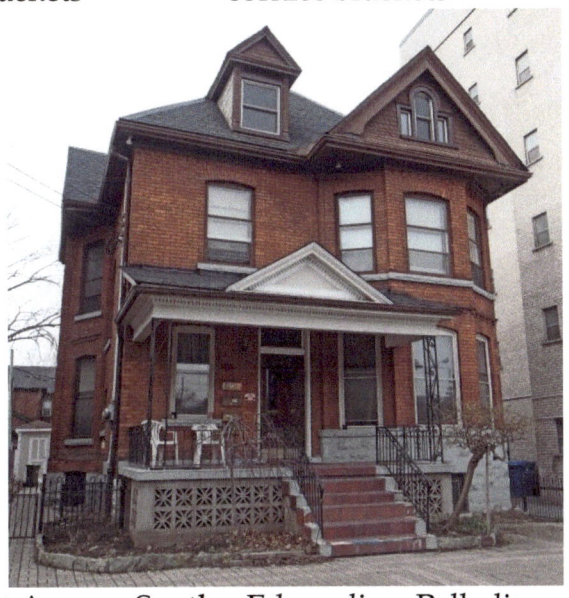

106 East Avenue South – Edwardian, Palladian window,
dormer, pediment, 2-storey bay window

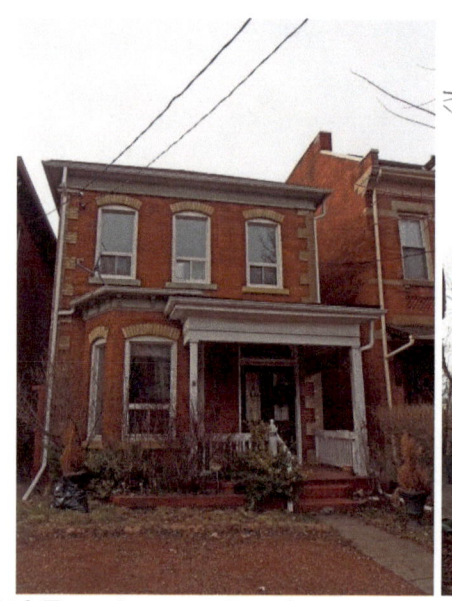

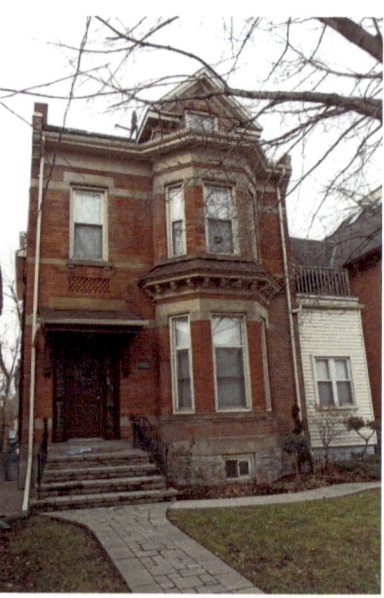

110 East Avenue South
Italianate, corner quoins

108 East Avenue South
2-storey bay window
banding

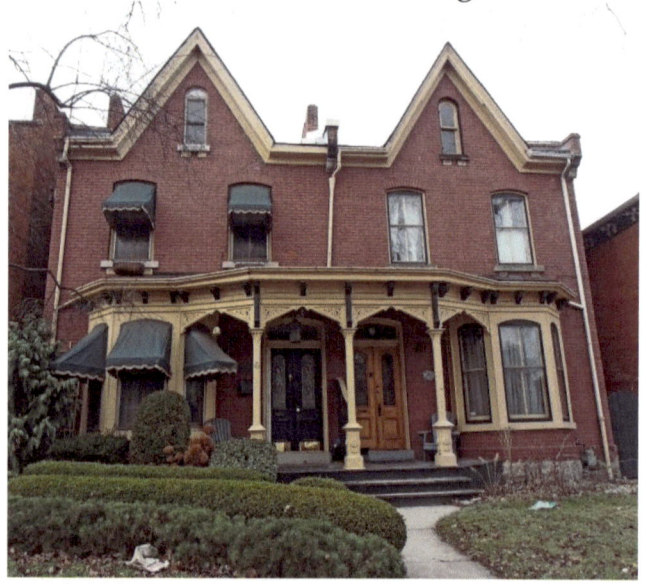

116-118 East Avenue South, Gothic Revival

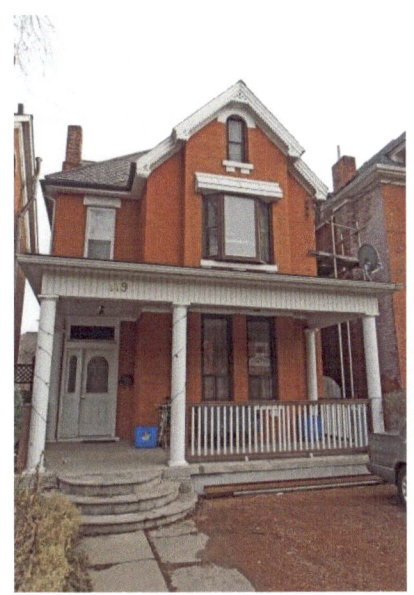
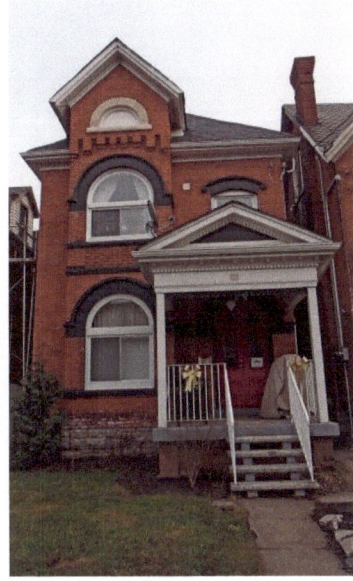

119 East Avenue South   121 East Avenue South

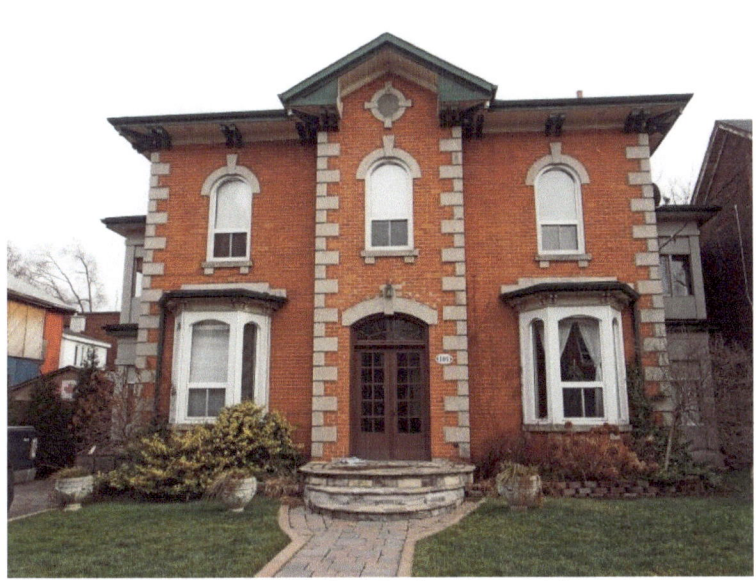

105 East Avenue South – Italianate with two-storey
frontispiece, bay windows, corner quoins, keystones

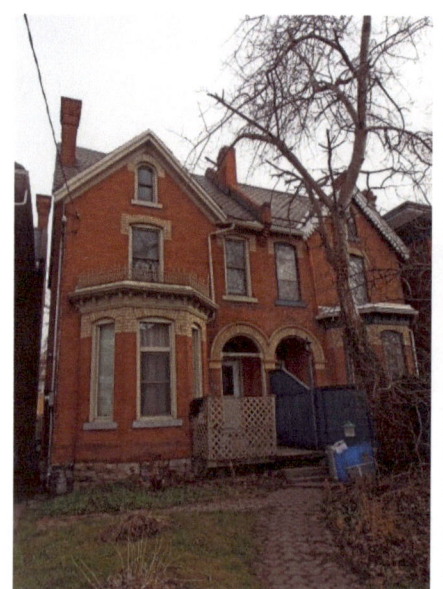 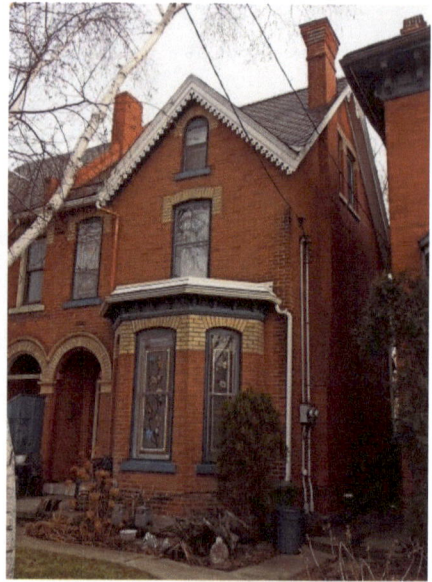

125 East Avenue South   127 East Avenue South
Gothic Revival, bay windows, verge board trim on gables

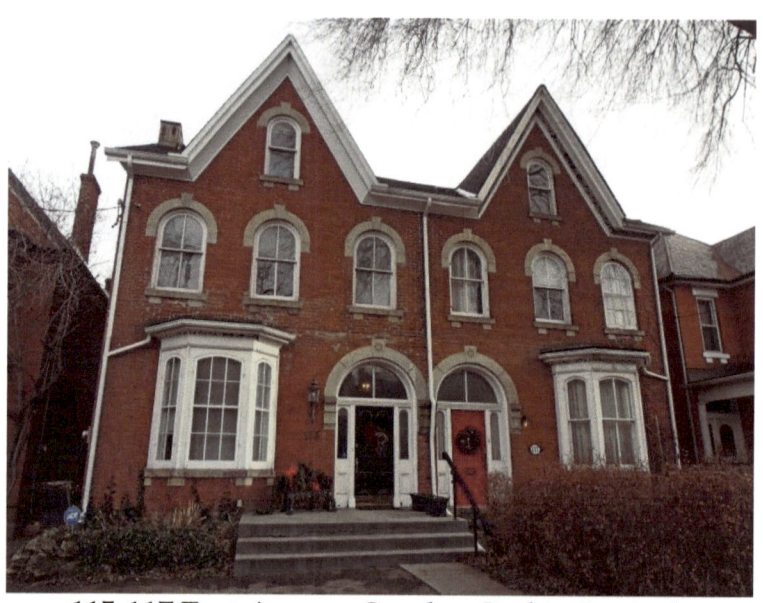

115-117 East Avenue South – Gothic Revival,
arched window voussoirs and keystones, bay windows

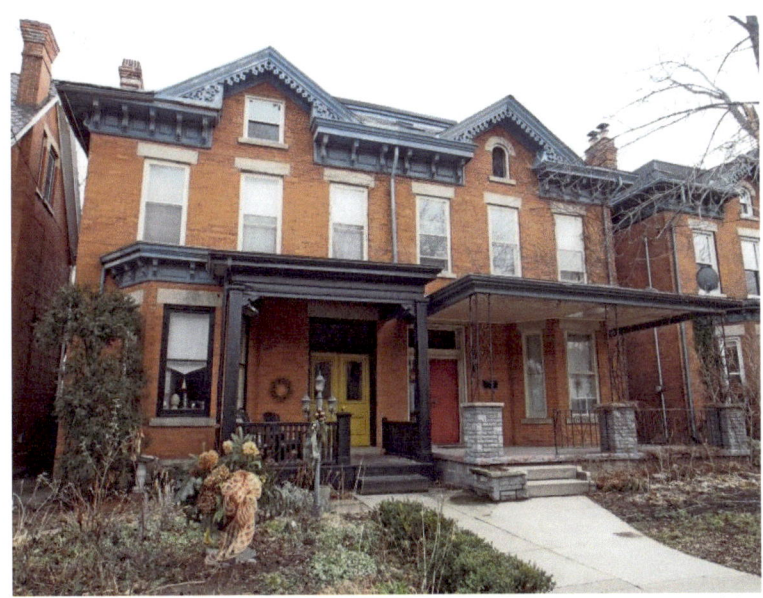

129-131 East Avenue South, verge board trim on gable, cornice brackets, bay window

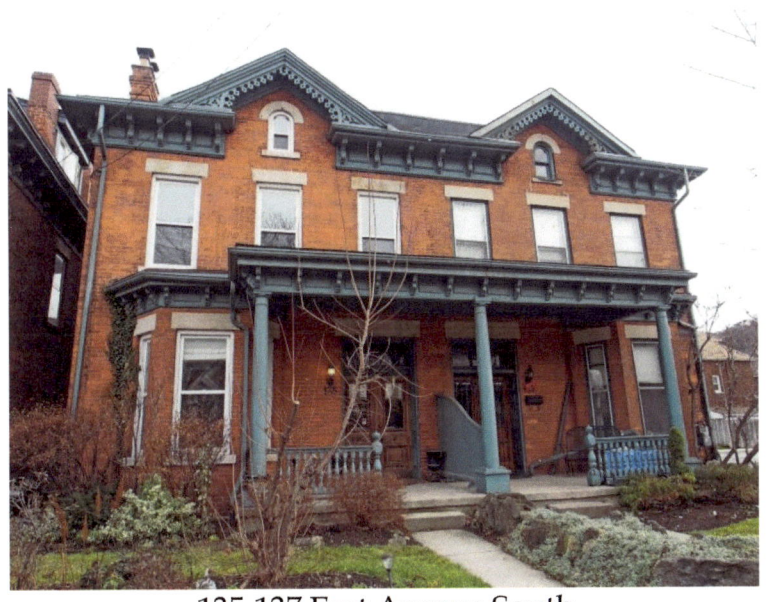

135-137 East Avenue South

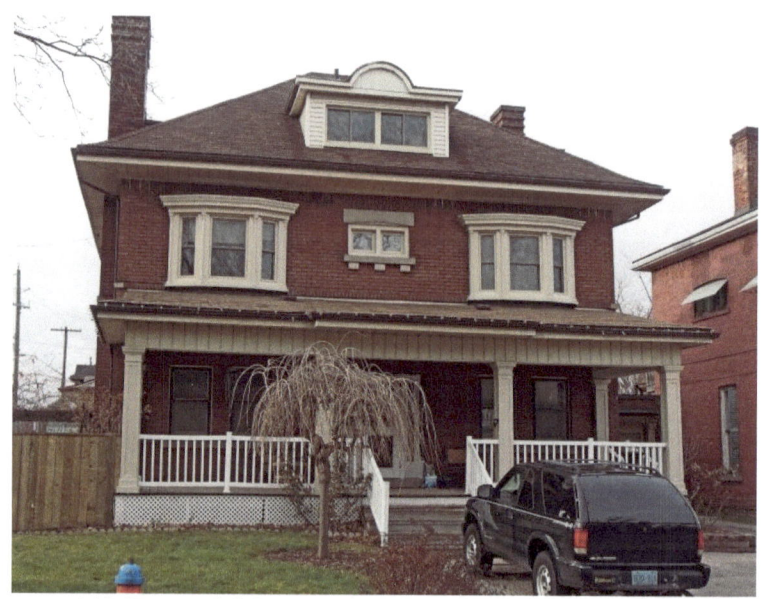

148 Emerald Street South – Italianate, dormer

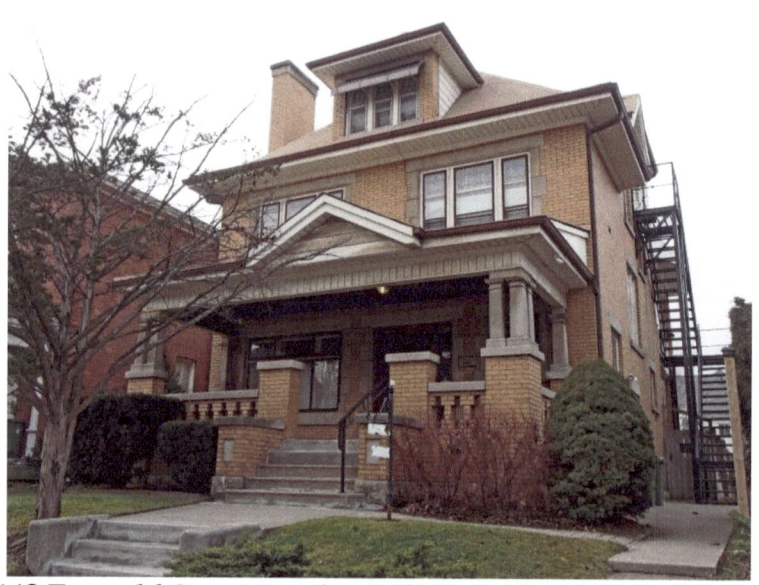

142 Emerald Street South – Italianate, dormer, pediment

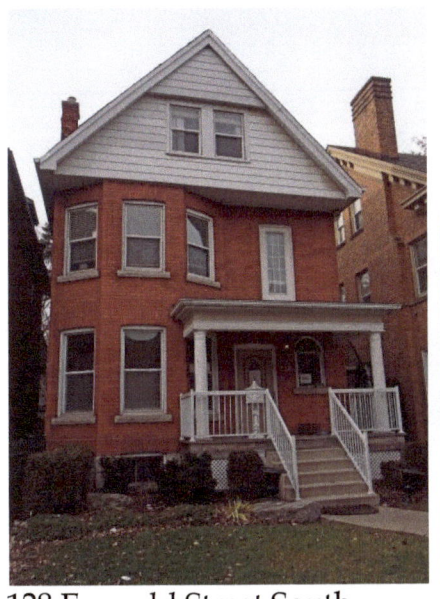

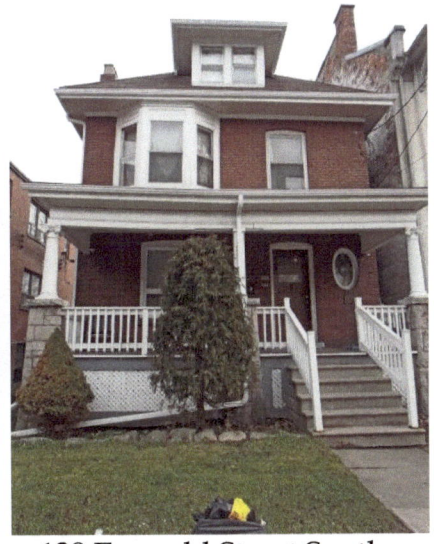

128 Emerald Street South
Edwardian
Two-storey bay window

129 Emerald Street South
Italianate, dormer

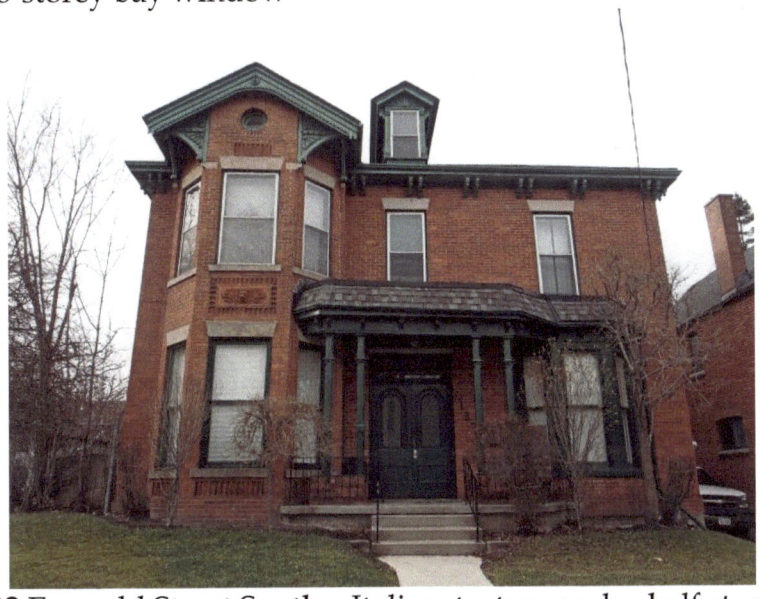

132 Emerald Street South – Italianate, two-and-a-half storey tower-like bay window, dormer in attic, paired cornice brackets, fretwork, patterned brickwork

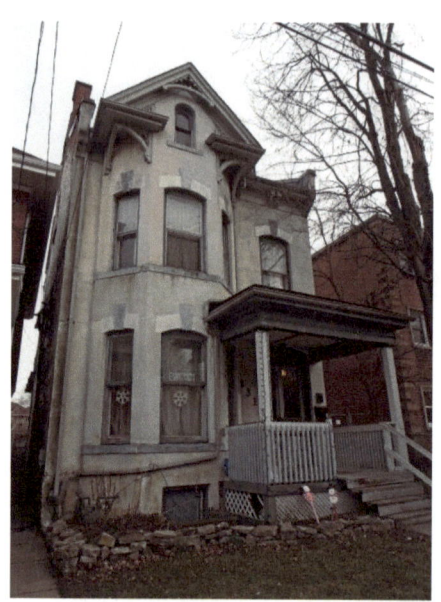

131 Emerald Street South

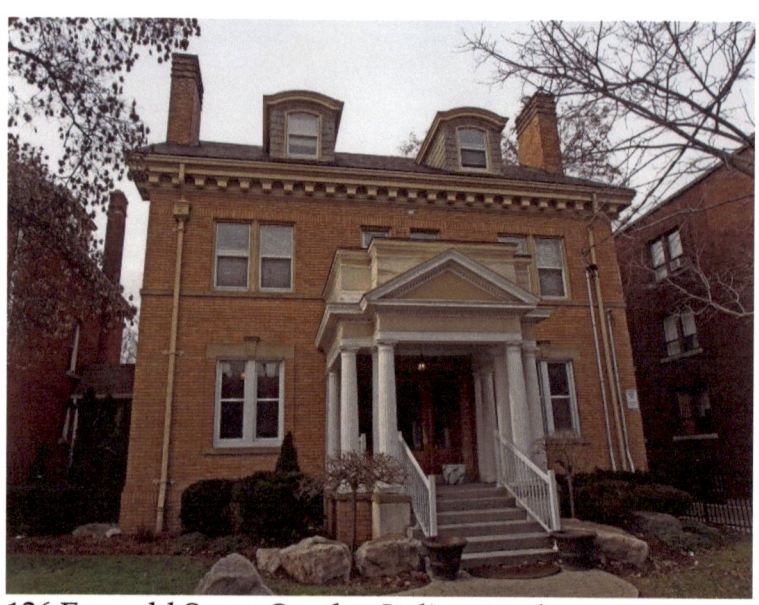

126 Emerald Street South – Italianate, dormers in attic, cornice brackets, pediment above porch

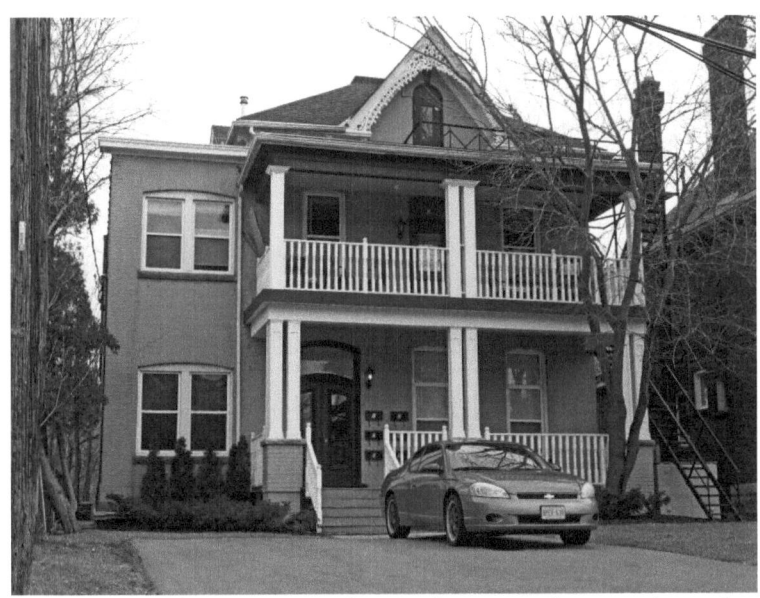

145 Emerald Street South – Italianate, dormer in attic, verandah on second floor

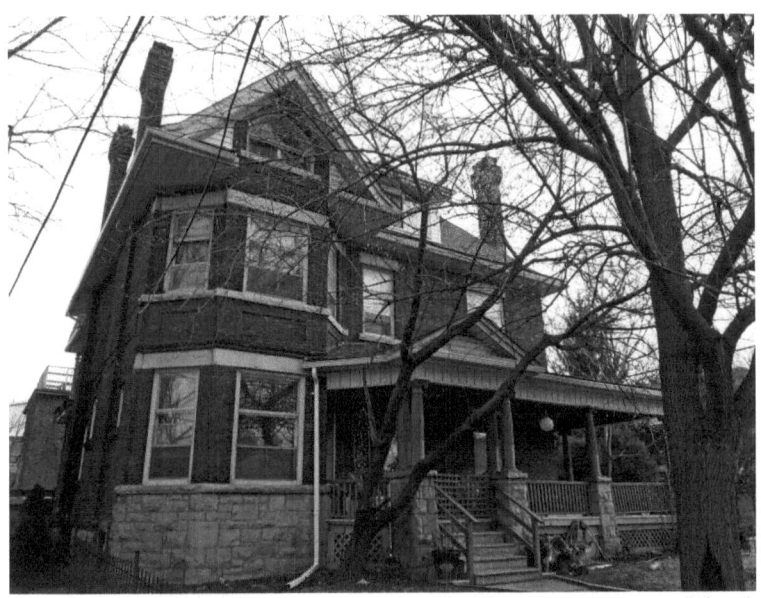

Emerald Street South – two-and-a-half storey tower-like bay, dormer, hipped roof

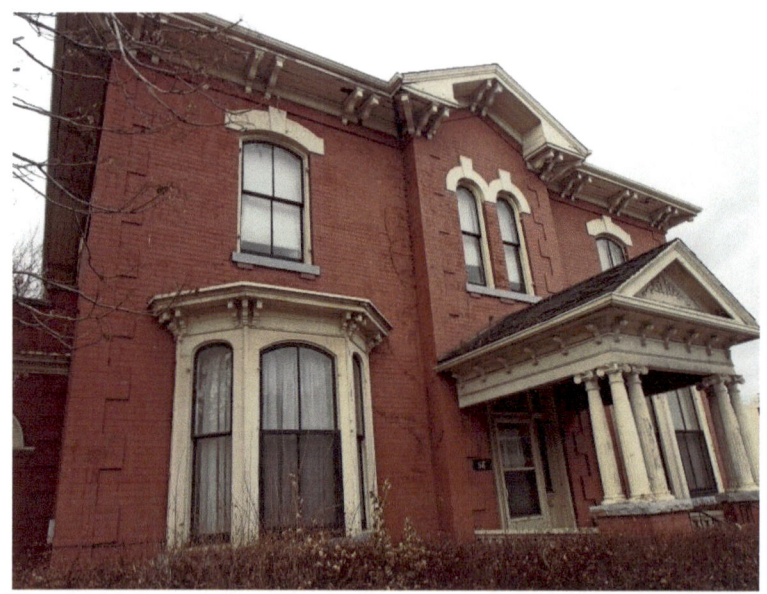

58 Emerald Street South – Italianate, two-storey frontispiece, pediment, Ionic capitals on pillars, bay window, cornice brackets

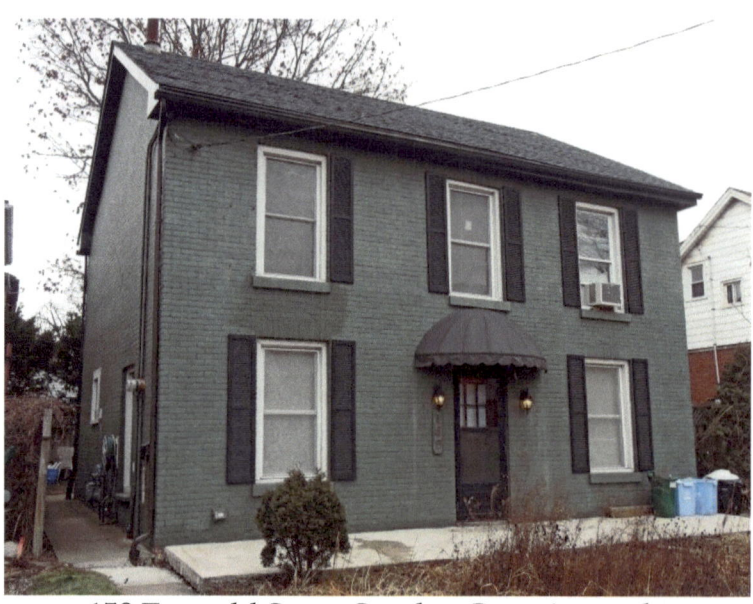

159 Emerald Street South – Georgian style

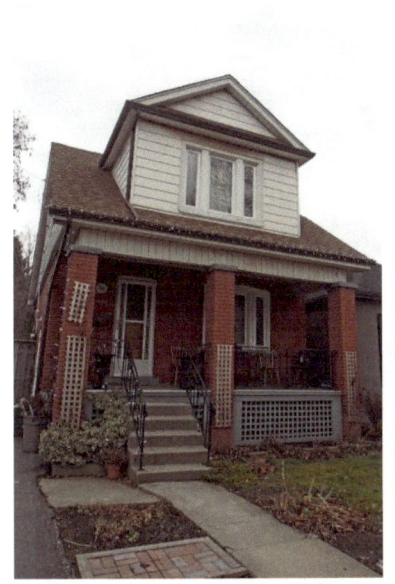

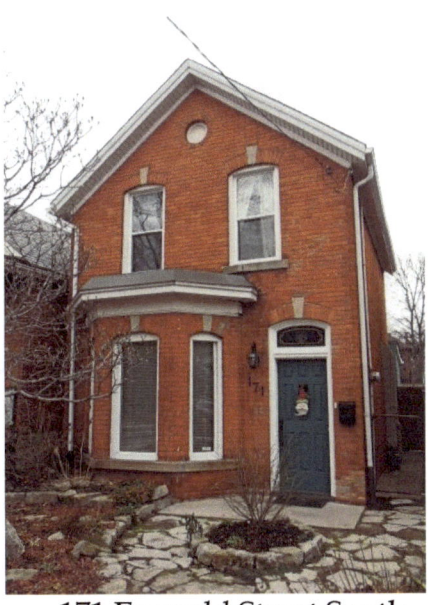

163 Emerald Street South
Large dormer in attic

171 Emerald Street South
Gothic Revival, bay window

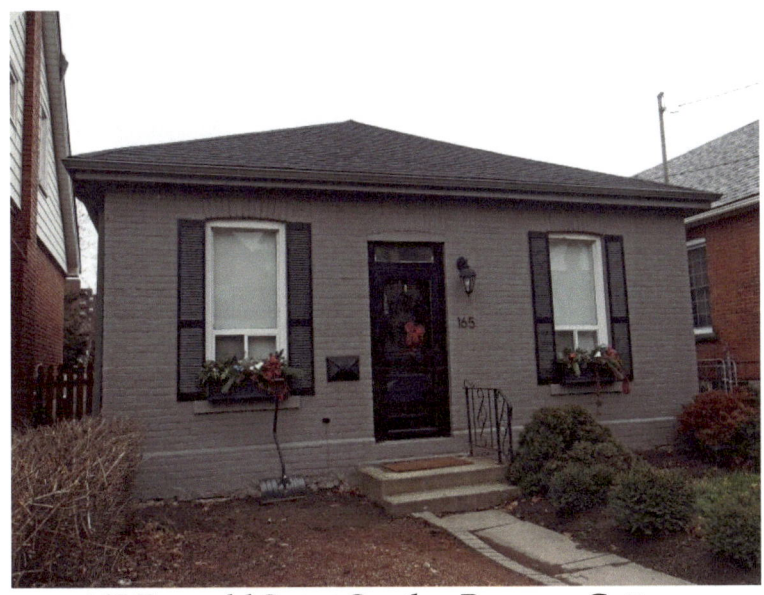

165 Emerald Street South – Regency Cottage

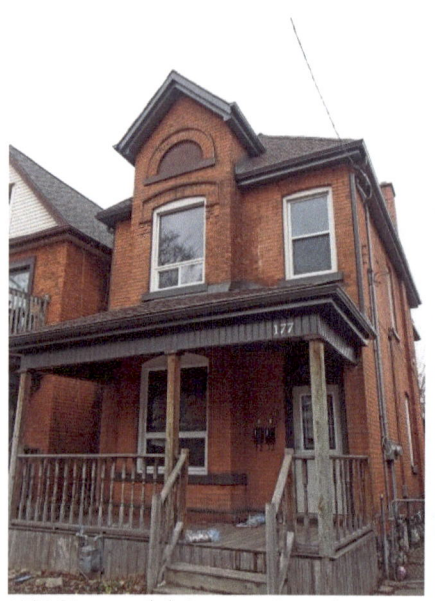

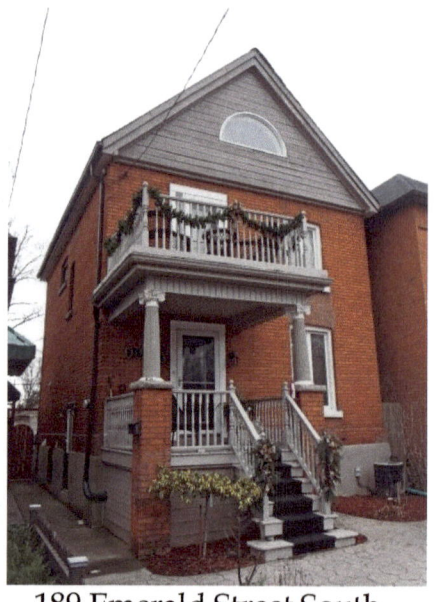

177 Emerald Street South
2½-storey frontispiece

189 Emerald Street South
Gothic Revival, Ionic capitals
Balcony on second floor

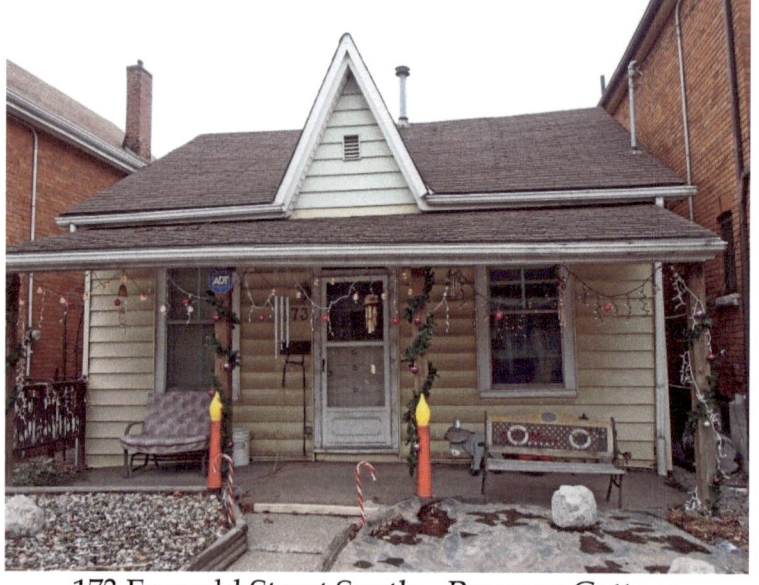

173 Emerald Street South – Regency Cottage

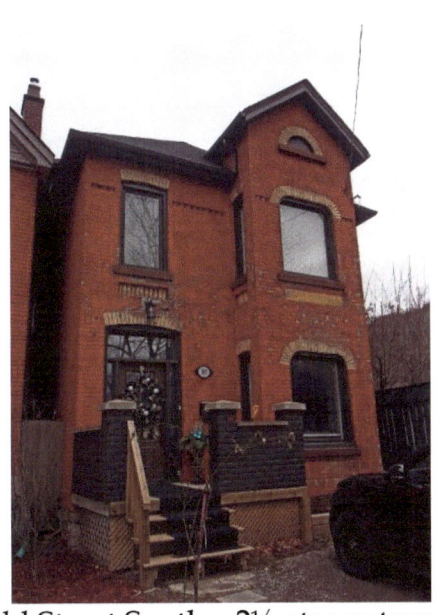

195 Emerald Street South – 2½-storey tower-like bay, dichromatic brickwork, dentil moulding

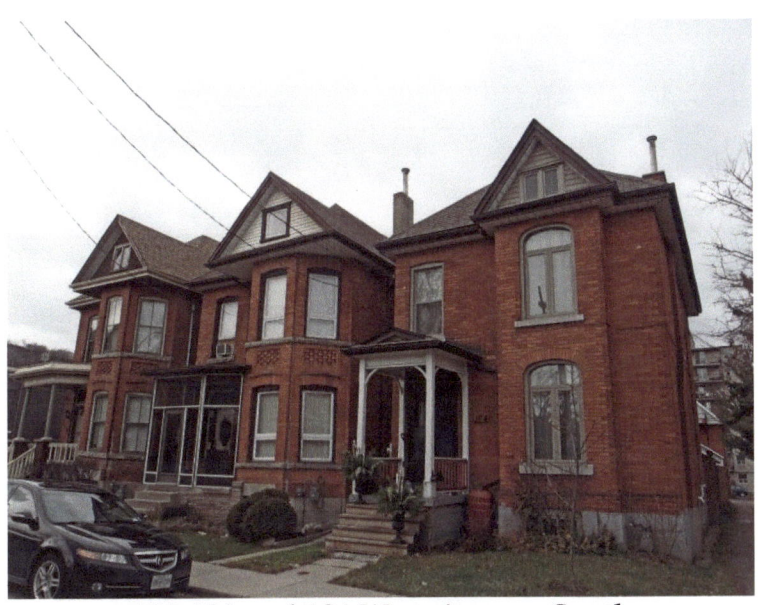

108-106 and 104 West Avenue South
Two-storey bay windows   two-storey frontispiece
Attic dormers

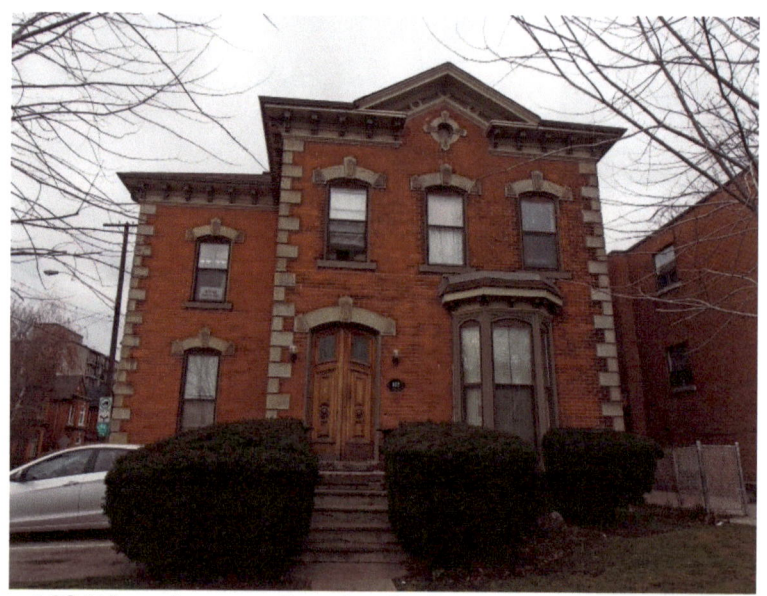

102 West Avenue South – Italianate, corner quoins, dichromatic brickwork, decorative keystones, cornice brackets

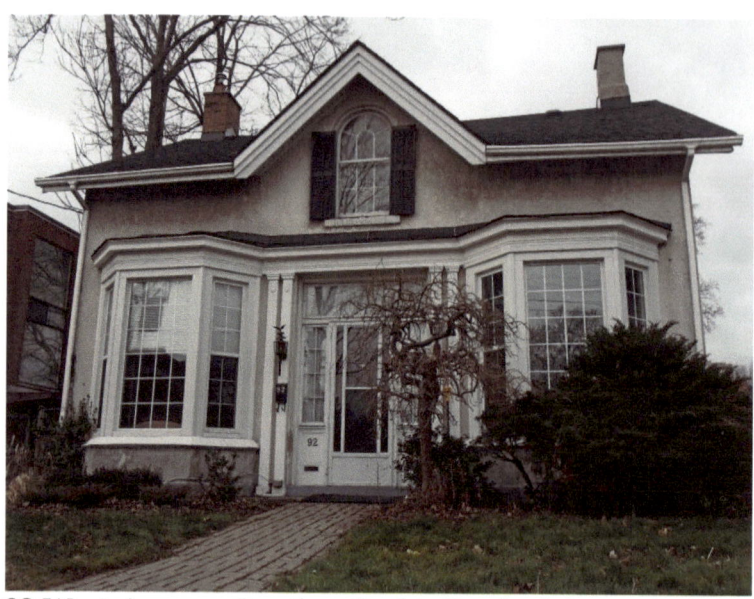

92 West Avenue South – Gothic Revival, bay windows

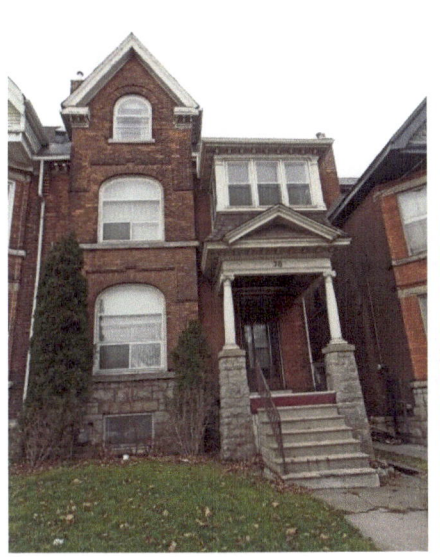

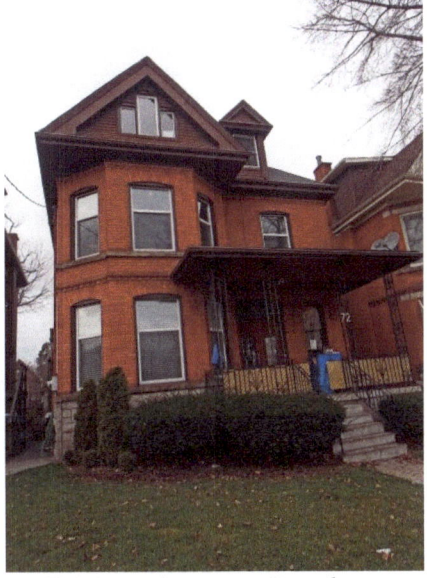

76 West Avenue South
Cornice return on gable
Pediment

72 West Avenue South
Edwardian, dormer
Palladian window

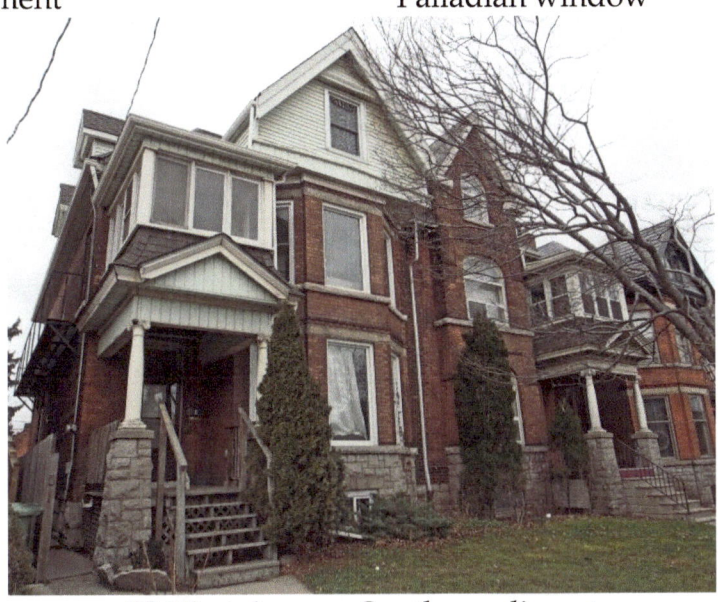

78 West Avenue South - pediment

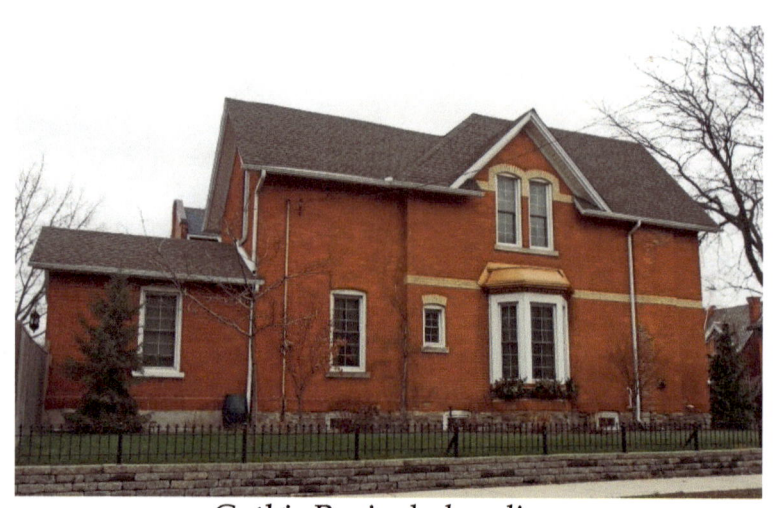

Gothic Revival - banding

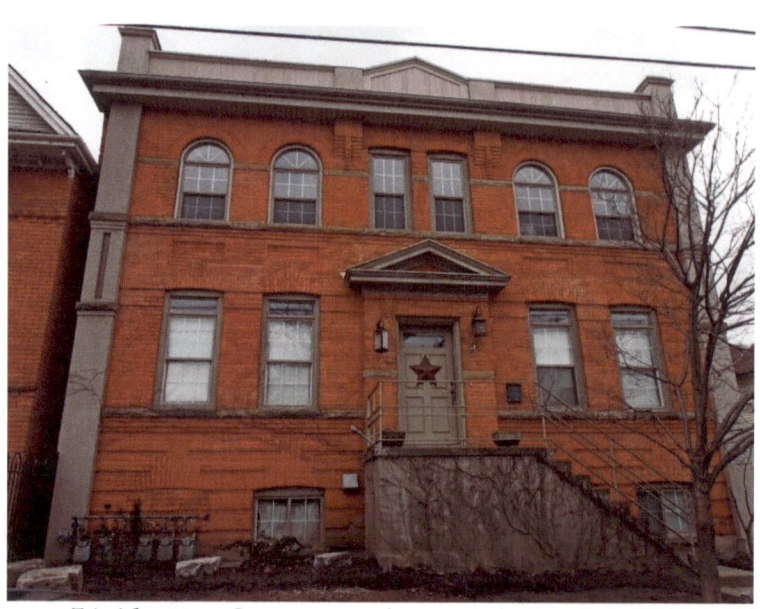

54 Alanson Street – pediment above entrance

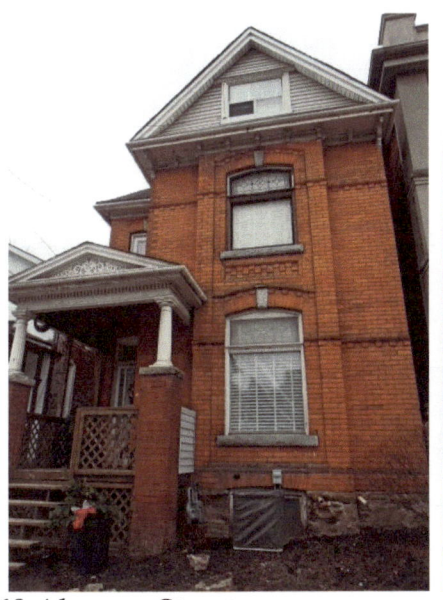

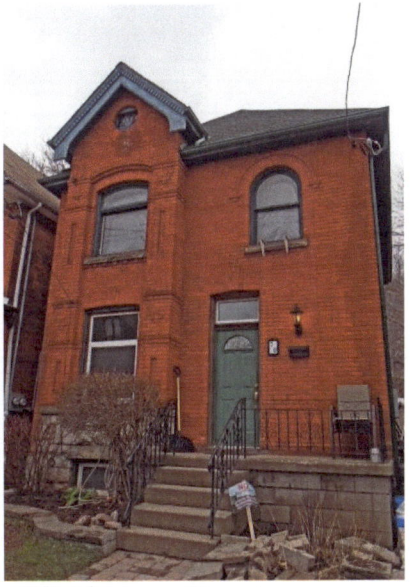

60 Alanson Street
Edwardian, pediment
2 storey frontispiece

70 Alanson Street
2½-storey frontispiece

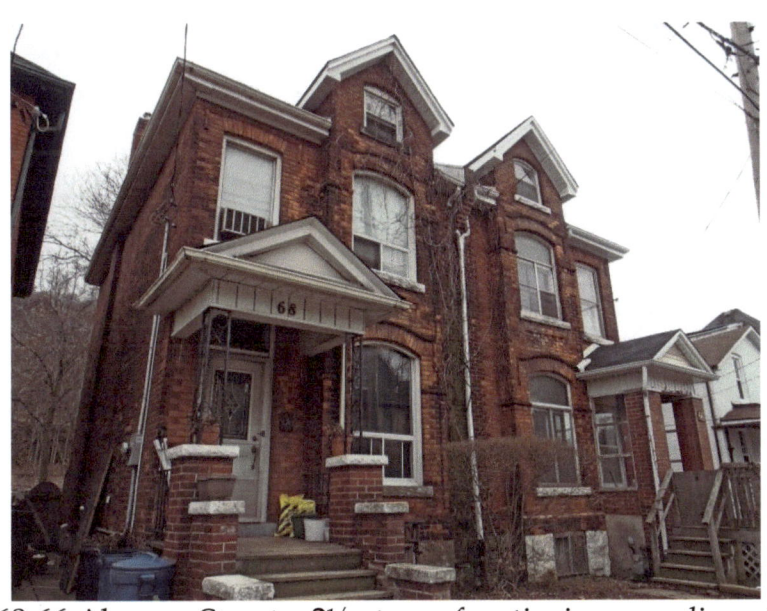

68-66 Alanson Street – 2½-storey frontispieces, pediment

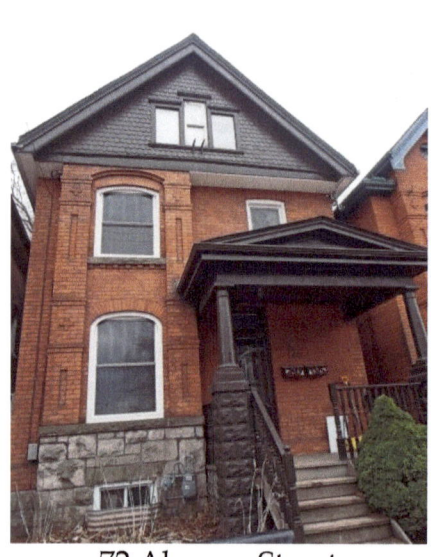

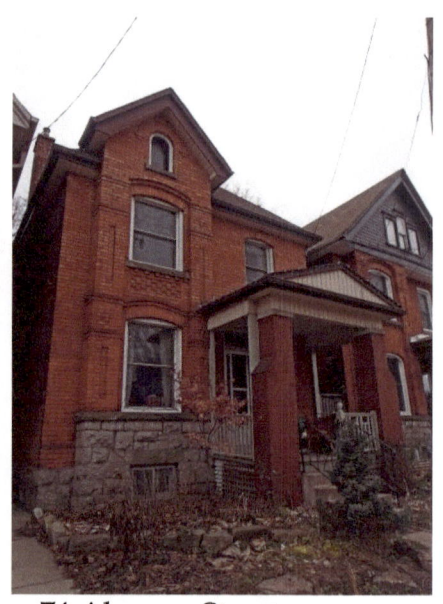

72 Alanson Street
Edwardian, Palladian window
Pediment

74 Alanson Street
2½-storey frontispiece,
pediment

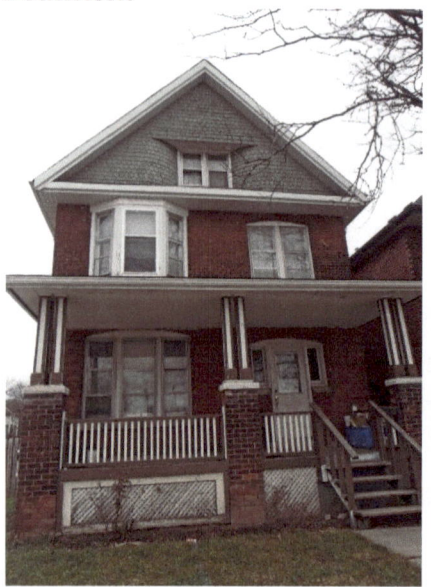

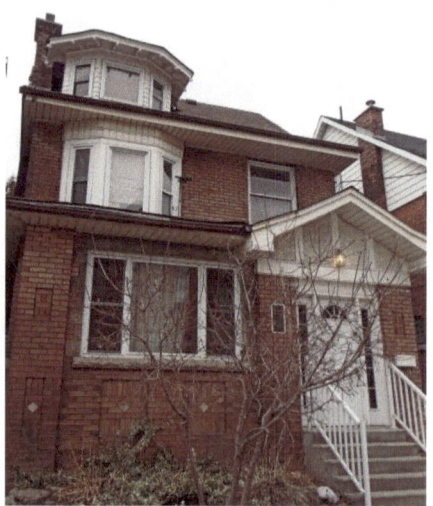

Ontario Avenue
Edwardian

136 Ontario Avenue

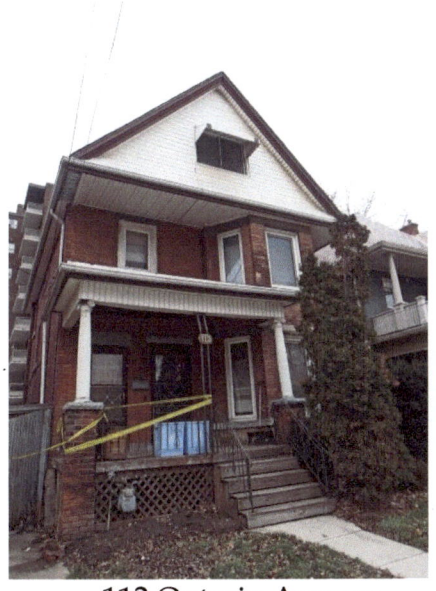

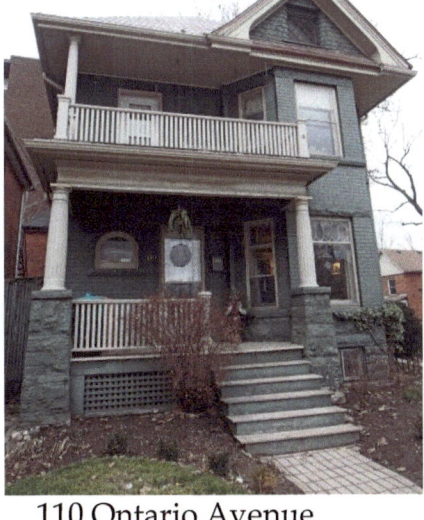

112 Ontario Avenue   110 Ontario Avenue

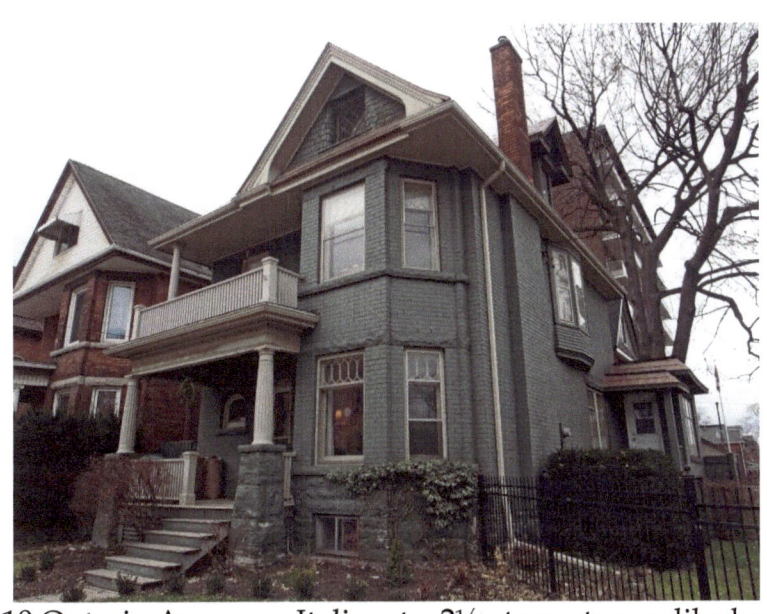

110 Ontario Avenue – Italianate, 2½-storey tower-like bay,
dormer on roof on side of building

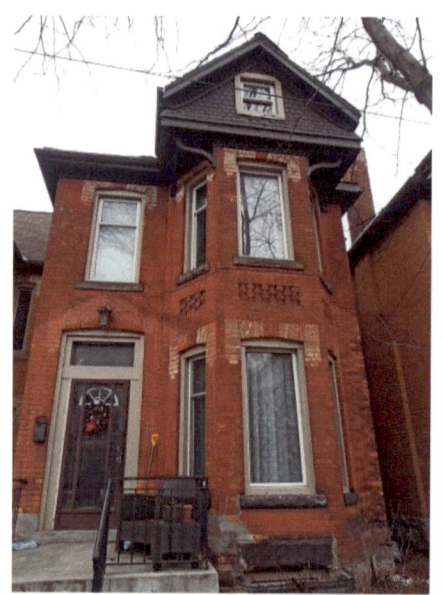

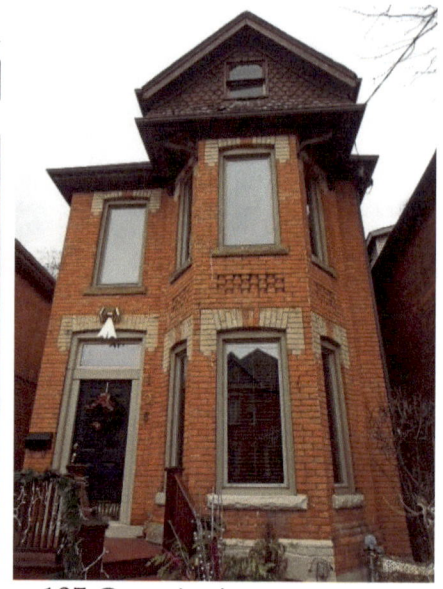

Ontario Avenue   105 Ontario Avenue

2½-storey tower-like bays

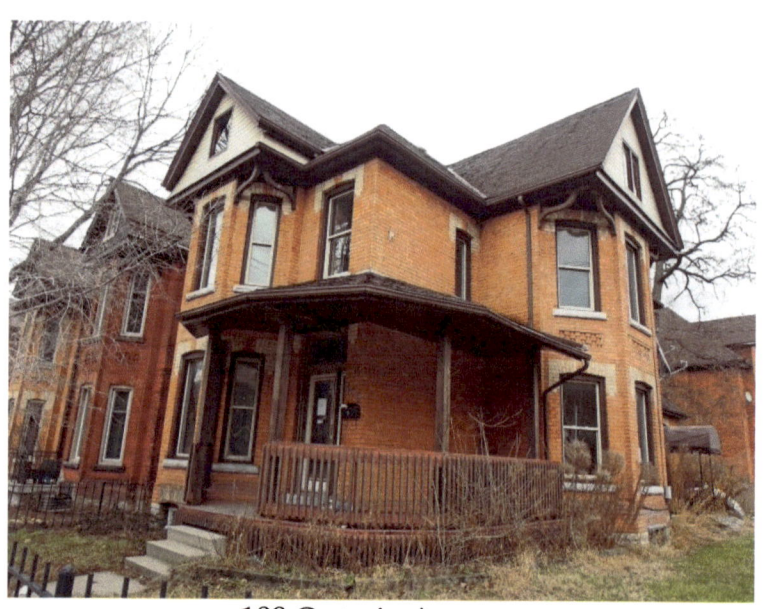

109 Ontario Avenue

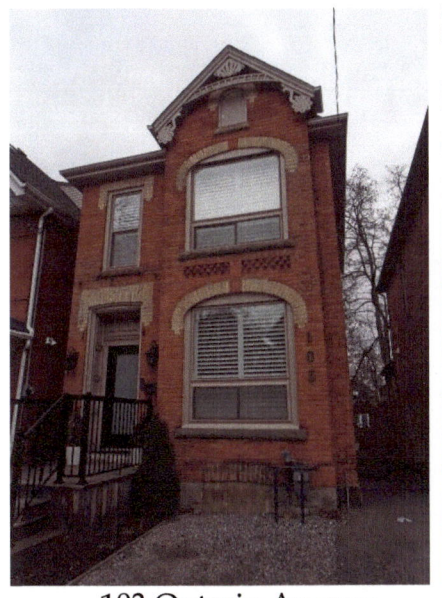

103 Ontario Avenue
Verge board trim on gable
Romanesque style window arches

93 Ontario Avenue

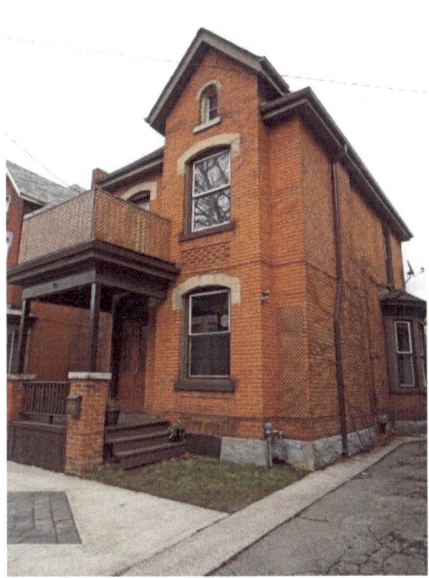

89 Ontario Avenue

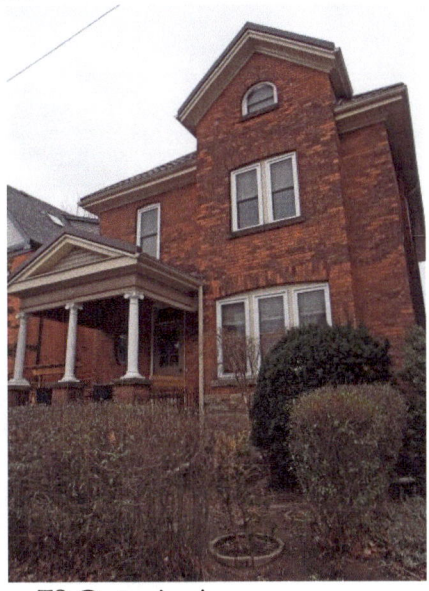

79 Ontario Avenue –
pediment, Ionic capitals

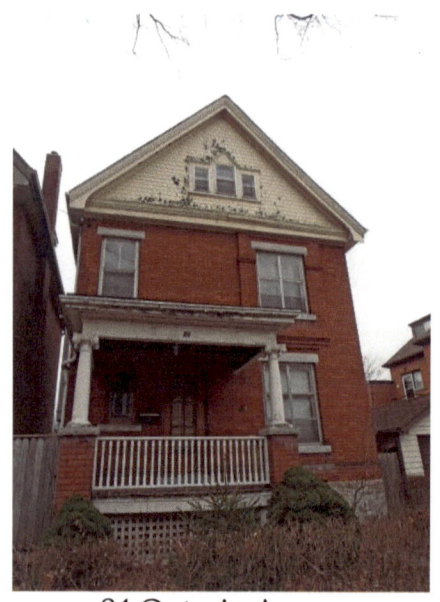

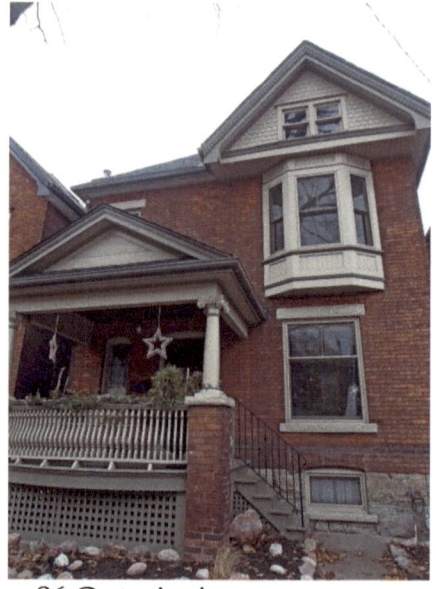

84 Ontario Avenue
Edwardian, Palladian window

86 Ontario Avenue
pediment, 2nd-storey bay

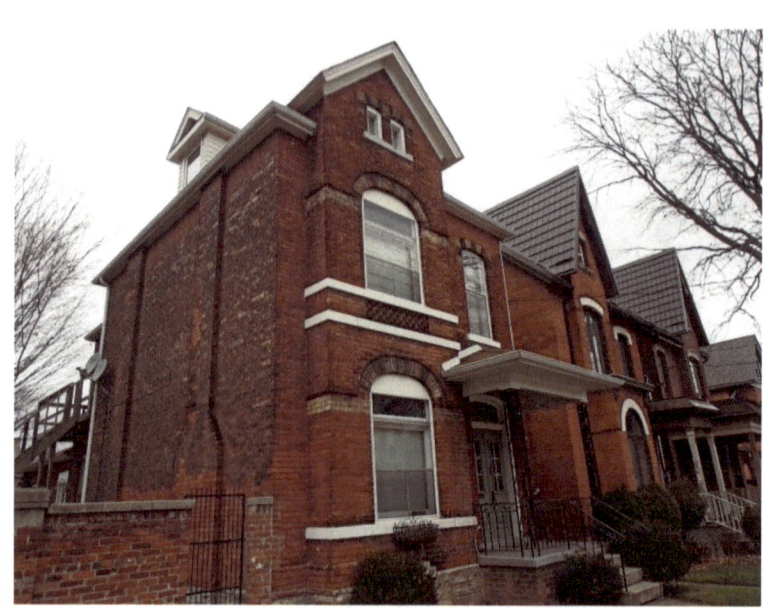

72 Ontario Avenue – Italianate, hipped roof, dormer in attic,
two-and-a-half storey tower-like bay

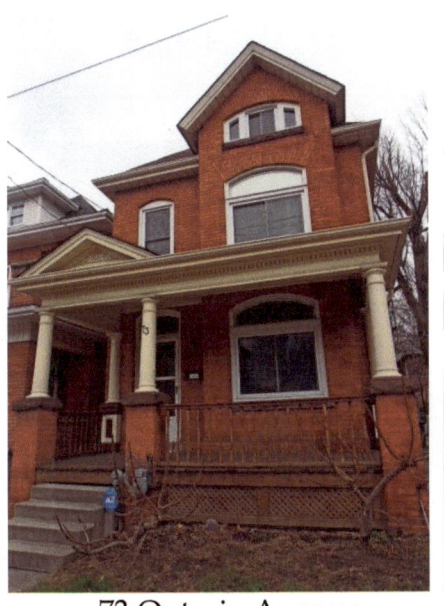

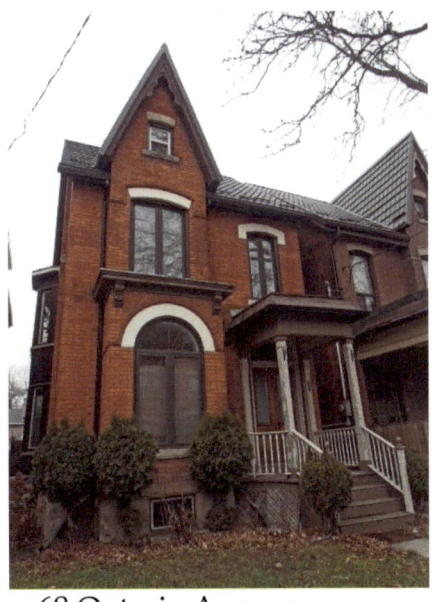

73 Ontario Avenue
Pediment

68 Ontario Avenue
Gothic Revival,
Romanesque style window arch

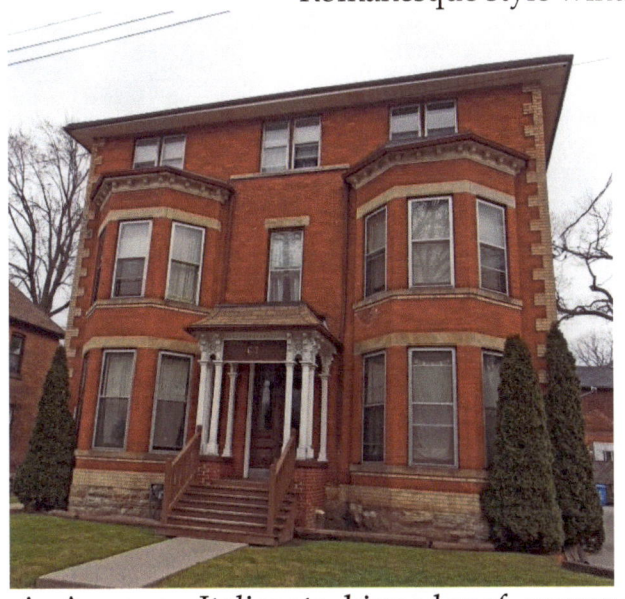

67 Ontario Avenue – Italianate, hipped roof, corner quoins,
two-storey bay windows

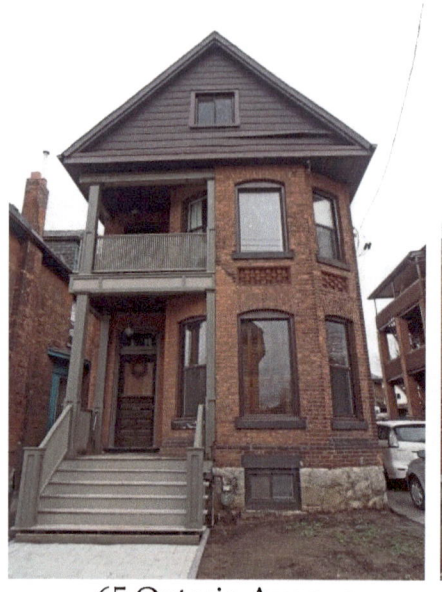 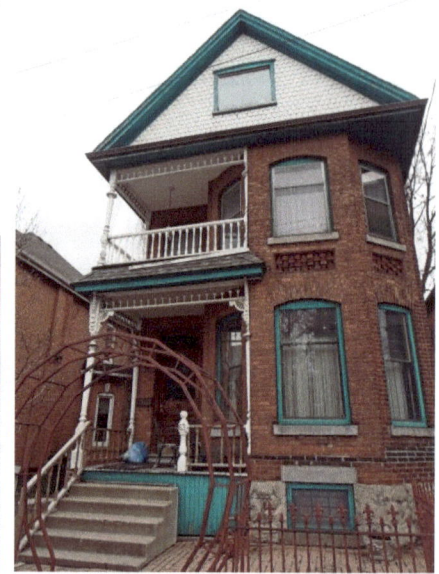

65 Ontario Avenue   63 Ontario Avenue

Edwardian, 2nd floor balcony

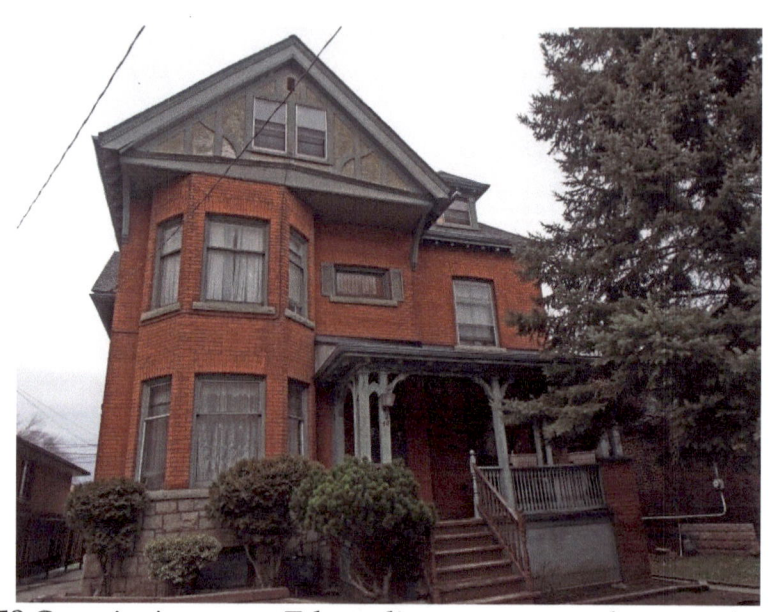

58 Ontario Avenue – Edwardian, two-storey bay window

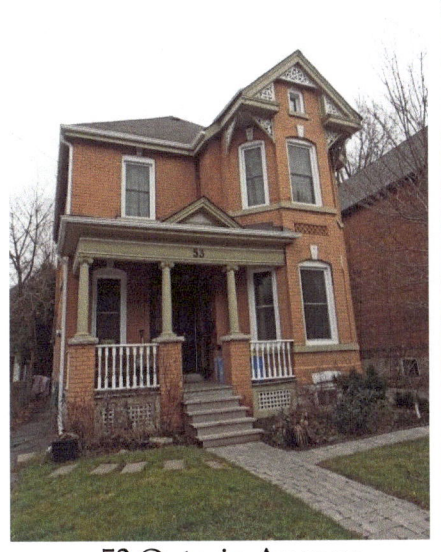

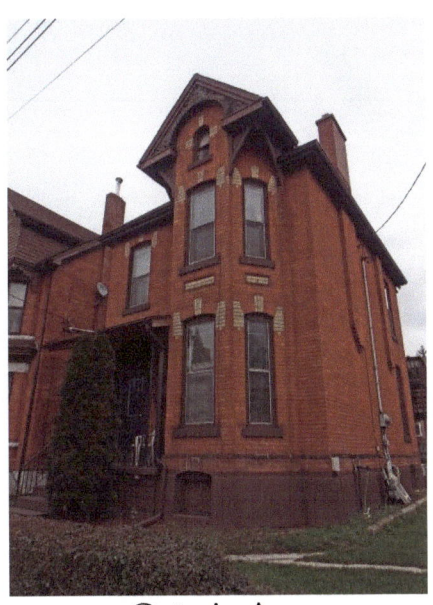

53 Ontario Avenue
Verge board trim, pediment,
Fretwork, Ionic capitals on pillars

Ontario Avenue
fretwork, keystones

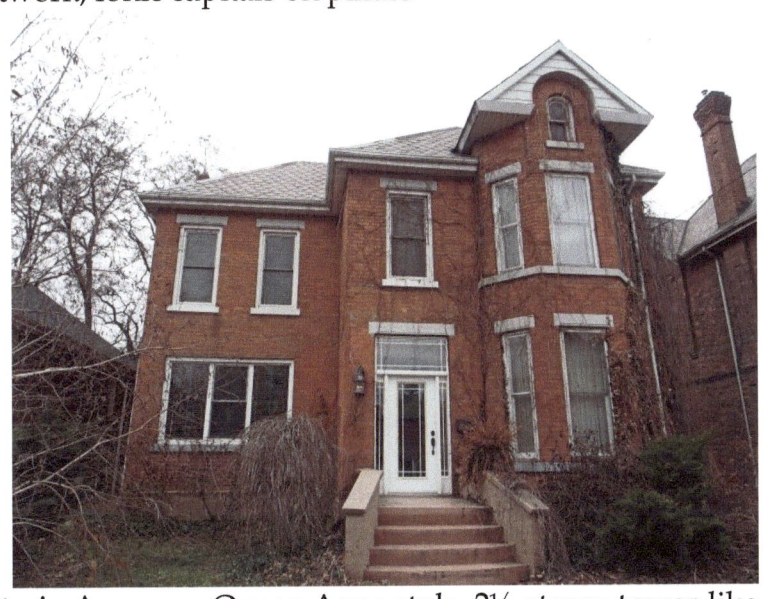

Ontario Avenue – Queen Anne style, 2½-storey tower-like bay

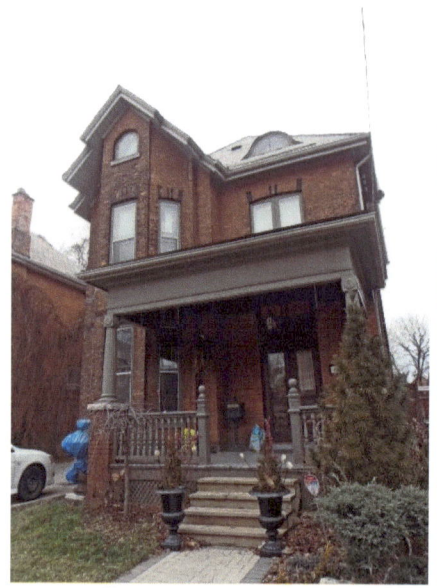

Ontario Avenue

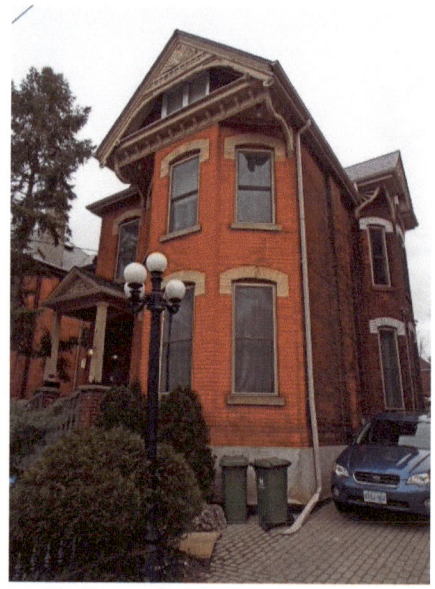

41 Ontario Avenue

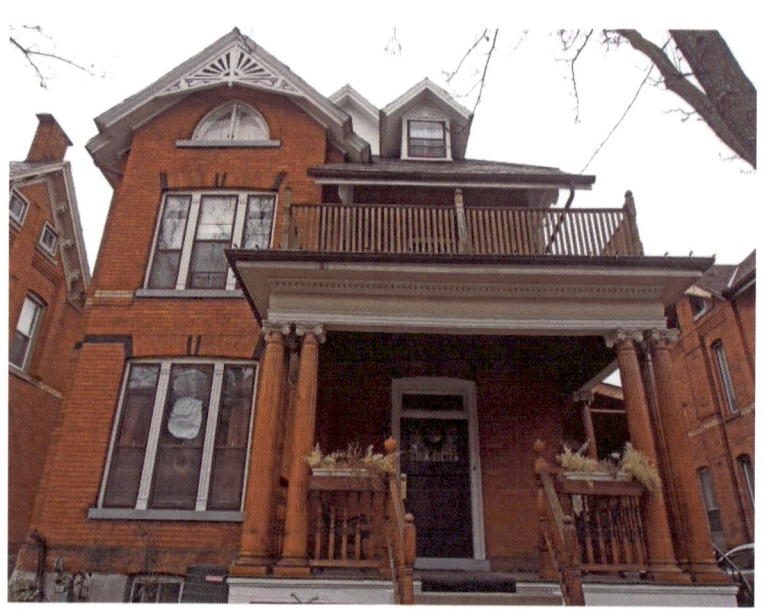

Ontario Avenue – Ionic capitals on pillars, second floor balcony, dormer, verge board trim on gable

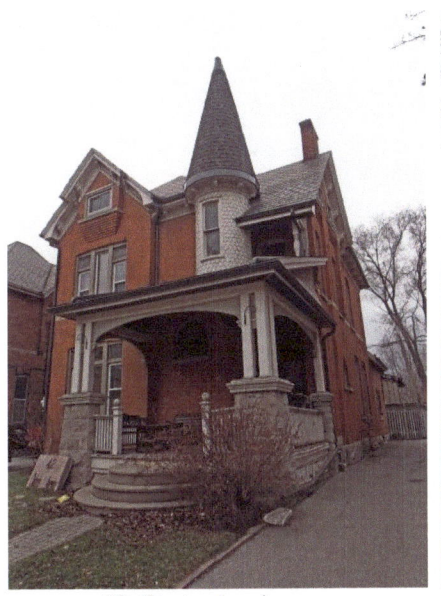

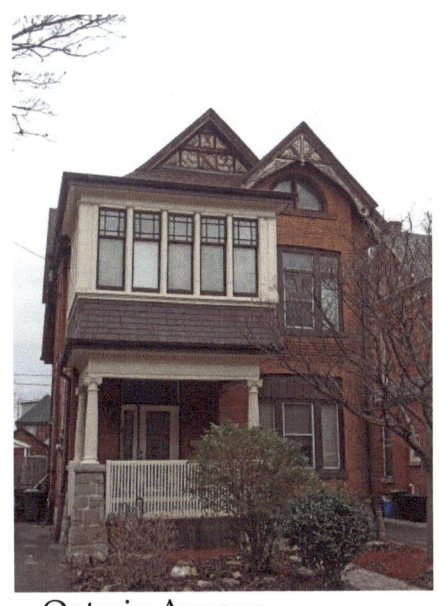

42 Ontario Avenue
Queen Anne, turret

Ontario Avenue
verge board trim

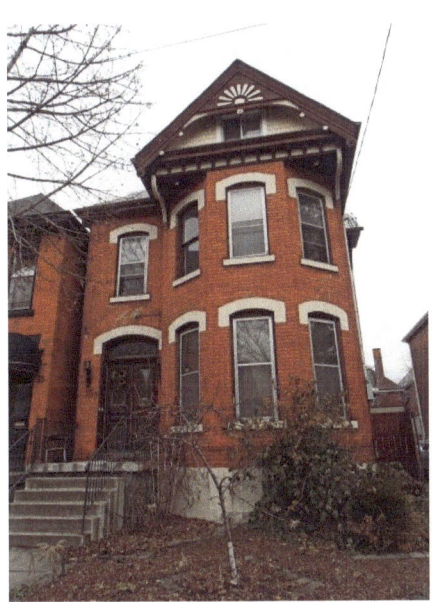

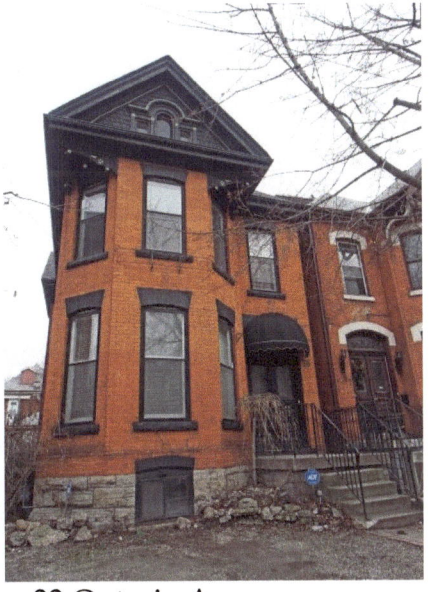

37 Ontario Avenue
Edwardian
Verge board trim on gable

33 Ontario Avenue
Edwardian, fretwork,
Palladian window

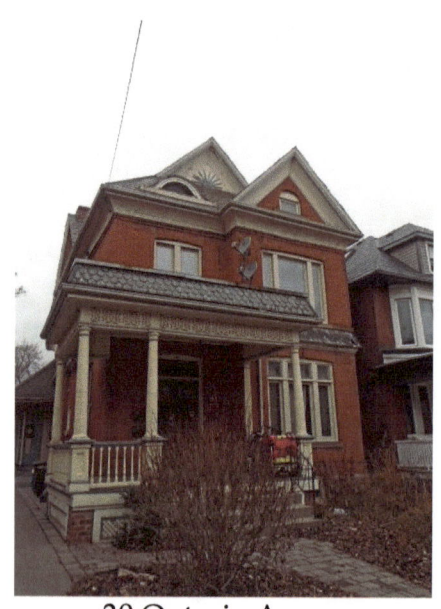

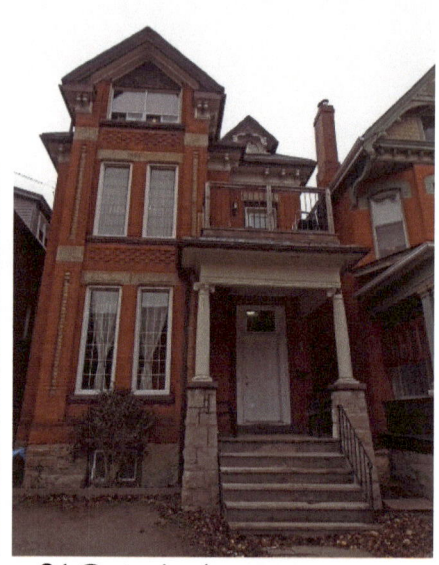

30 Ontario Avenue
Queen Anne

24 Ontario Avenue
Ionic capitals

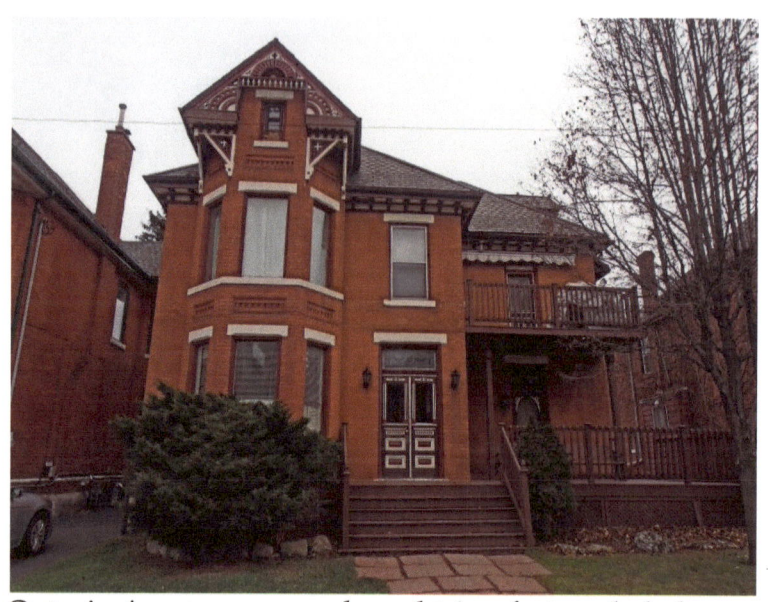

Ontario Avenue – verge board trim, fretwork, balcony,
2½-storey tower like bay

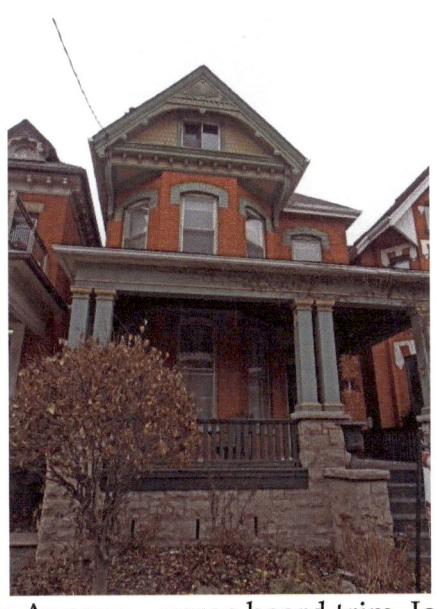

19 Ontario Avenue – verge board trim, Ionic pillars

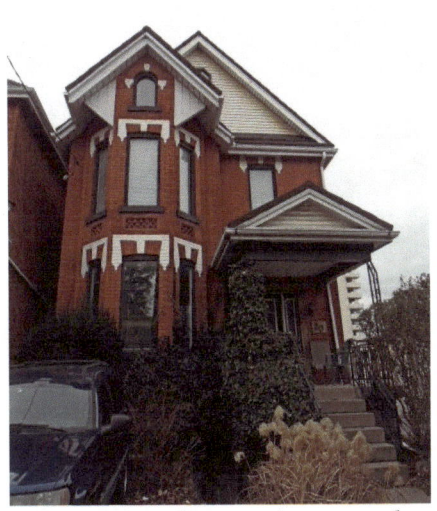

20 Ontario Avenue – Queen Anne style, pediment

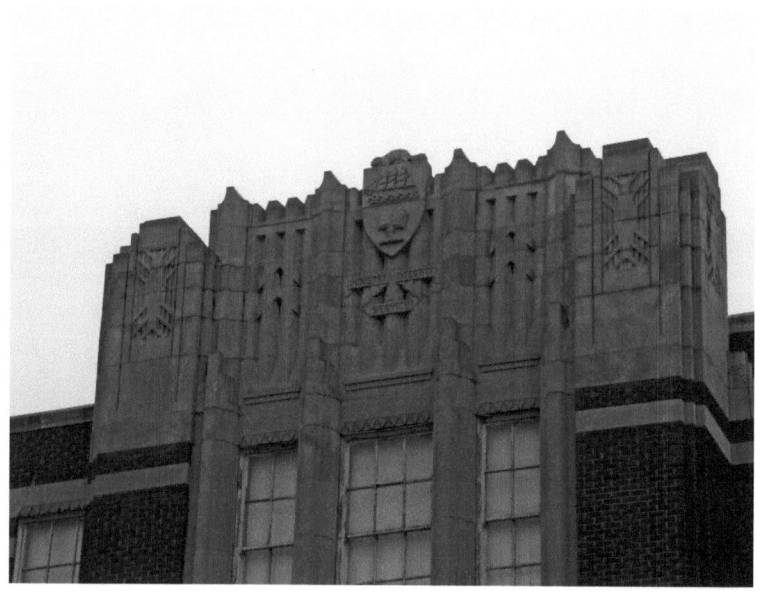

Sanford Avenue Public School – Industry, Integrity, Service
Erected A.D. 1932 – Art Deco style

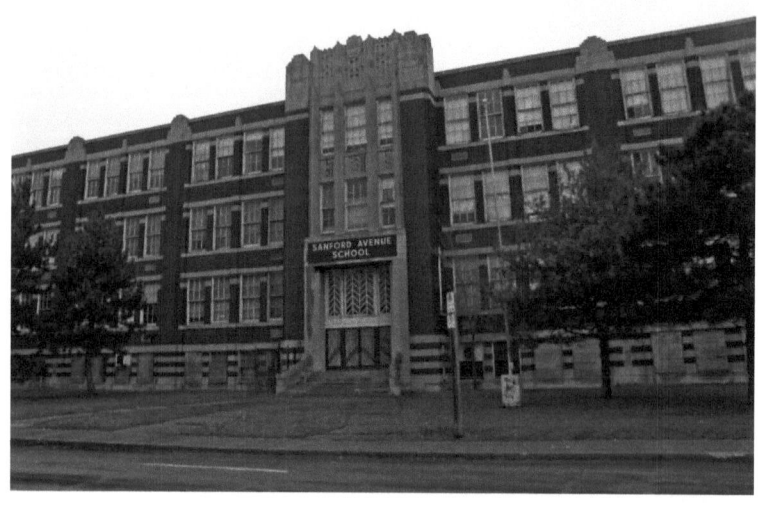

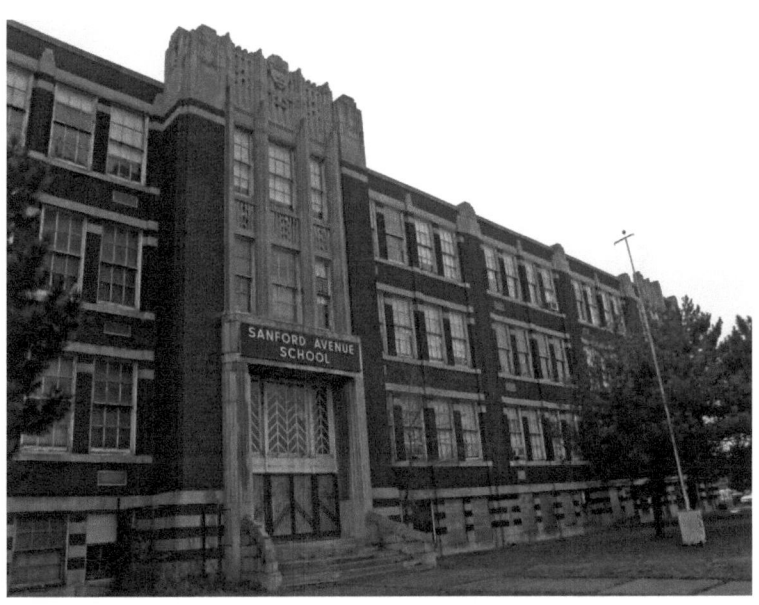

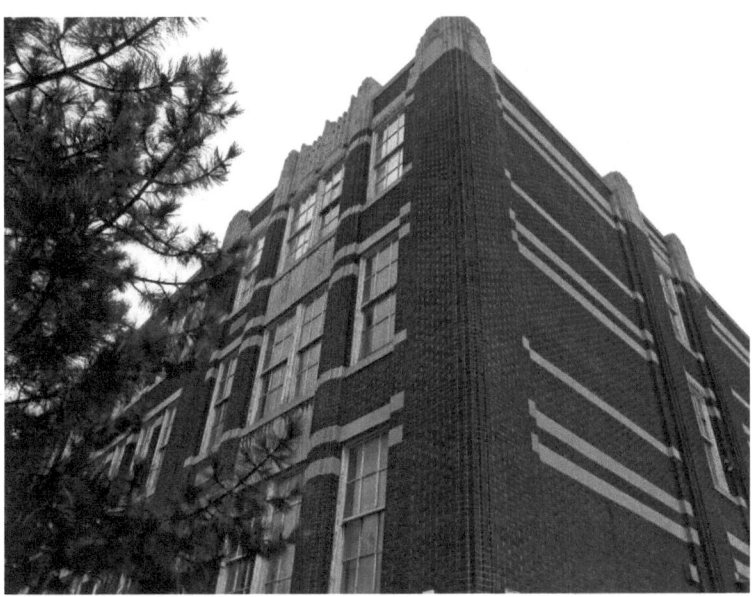

Banding: Different materials, colours or textures used in horizontal bands along a wall. Example: 136 East Avenue South	
Brackets: a decorative or weight-bearing structural element which forms a right angle with one side against a wall and the other under a projecting surface such as an eave or roof. Example: 58 Emerald Street South	
Buttress: a masonry structure built against or projecting from a wall which serves to support or reinforce the wall. In Canadian architecture, they are sometimes used for decoration. Example: 475 Mary Street	
Capital: The uppermost finish or decoration on a column. An Ionic column has a small base, a thin elegant shaft, and a capital composed of volutes which are carved whirls or twists that take the form of a scroll. Example: 109 East Avenue South	 Ionic
Cornice Return: decorative element on the end of a gable. Example: 122 East Avenue South	
Dentil Moulding: an even series of rectangles used as ornamental decoration in cornices. Example: 475 Mary Street	

Dichromatic brickwork: the use of two colours of brick, tile or slate to decorate a façade. Example: 158-160 Simcoe Street East	
Dormer: (French for "sleep") a gable end window that pierces through the plane of a sloping roof surface to create usable space in the top floor or attic of a building by adding headroom. Example: 126 Emerald Street South	
Fretwork: interlaced decorative design resembling a bracket Example: 132 Emerald Street South	
Gable: the triangular portion of a wall between the edges of a sloping roof. Example: 15 Victoria Avenue North	
Keystones and Voussoirs: a voussoir is a wedge-shaped element used in building an arch. A keystone is the central stone that locks all the stones into position, allowing the arch to bear weight. A keystone is often enlarged and embellished. Example: 102 West Avenue South	

Mansard Roof: This style was popularized by Francois Mansart (1598-1666), an accomplished architect of the French Baroque period and especially fashionable during the Second French Empire (1852-1870). This roof is almost flat on the top section, with two slopes on each of its sides with the lower slope at a steeper angle than the upper and having dormer windows. Example: 90 Stinson Street	
Palladian Window: a large window that is divided into three sections with the centre section larger than the two side sections and usually arched. Example: 146 Stinson Street	
Pediment: a triangular section above the horizontal structure (entablature), typically supported by columns. The inside of the triangle is called the tympanum. Example: 109 East Avenue South	
Quoin: masonry blocks at the corner of a wall, often a decorative feature, usually larger or of a different colour than the rest of the wall. Example: 105 East Avenue South	
Relief: A sculpted frieze or band where the forms or designs project from the flat base. Example: 132 Emerald Street South	

Rose Window: a circular window with ornamental tracery radiating from the centre. Example: St. Lawrence the Martyr Parish Church, 475 Mary Street (corner of Picton)	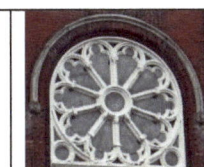
Sidelight: a window, usually with a vertical emphasis, that flanks a door, and is often used to emphasize the importance of a primary entrance. Example: 129 East Avenue South	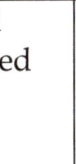 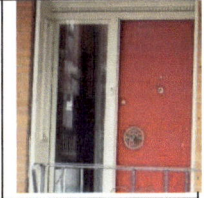
Transom Window: the light above the doorway, also called a fanlight. Example: 129 East Avenue South	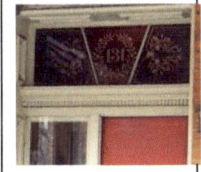
Turret: a small tower that projects from the wall of a building. Example: 42 Ontario Avenue	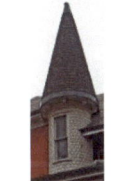
Verge board and Finial: also called bargeboards – hang from the projecting end of a roof and are often elaborately carved and ornamented. **Finial:** ornament added to the top of a gable, pinnacle, canopy or spire – a Gothic element. Example: 118 Stinson Street	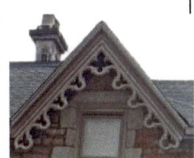

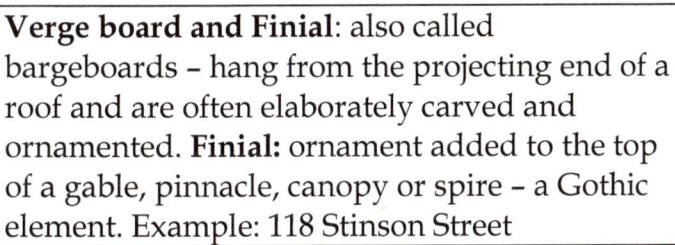

Building Styles

Art Deco, 1910-1940 - The Art Deco Style was developed for the French luxury market after World War I. Art Deco left its mark on everything from lamps and foot stools to purses and hair combs. The style was adopted in Ontario by wealthy and very fashionable patrons who wanted Art Deco detailing to make their buildings look lavish and exotic. Example: Sanford Avenue Public School	
Edwardian, 1900-1930 – This style bridges the ornate and elaborate styles of the Victorian era and the simplified styles of the 20th century. Balanced facades, simple roof lines, dormer windows, large front porches, and smooth brick surfaces are its characteristics. Example: 146 Stinson Street	
Georgian, before 1860 – This style began with the British King Georges in the 18th century. These buildings have balanced facades around a central door, medium-pitched gable roofs, and small paned windows. Example: 159 Emerald Street South	
Gothic Revival, 1830-1890 – These decorative buildings have sharply-pitched gables with highly detailed verge boards, pointed-arch window openings, and dichromatic brickwork. It is a common style in Ontario. Example: 136 East Avenue South	

Italianate, 1850-1900 – It has wide-bracketed eaves, belvederes, wrap-around verandahs. Example: 126 Emerald Street South	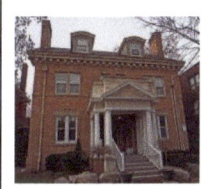
Queen Anne, 1885-1900 – This style is distinguished by an irregular outline featuring a combination of an offset tower, broad gables, projecting two-storey bays, verandahs, multi-sloped roofs, and tall, decorative chimneys. A mixture of brick and wood is common. Windows often have one large single-paned bottom sash and small panes in the upper sash. Example: 42 Ontario Avenue	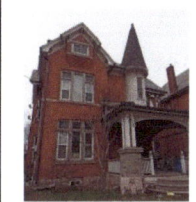
Romanesque Revival, 1880-1910 – This style hearkens back to medieval architecture of the 11th and 12th centuries with a heavy appearance, blocky towers and rounded arches. Example: 127 East Avenue South	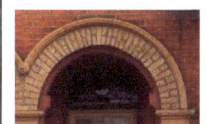